Drout's Qu[

Easy Old English

by Michael D.C. Drout
with Bruce D. Gilchrist
and Rachel Kapelle

Witan Publishing

CONTENTS

ACKNOWLEDGMENTS

For their inspired teaching, my sincere thanks to Peggy Knapp of Carnegie Mellon University, John Miles Foley of the Center for Studies in Oral Tradition at the University of Missouri-Columbia, Martin Camargo of the University of Illinois and Allen J. Frantzen of Loyola University Chicago.

My gratitude also goes out to my colleagues in the English department at Wheaton College: Deyonne Bryant, Claire Buck, Shawn Christian, Beverly Lyon Clark, Sam Coale, Katherine Conway, Susan Dearing, Paula Krebs, Lisa Lebduska, Charlotte Meehan, Dick Pearce, Sheila Shaw, Pam Stafford, Josh Stenger, Sue Standing and Kathleen Vogt. Thanks also to Provosts Susanne Woods, Molly Easo Smith and Linda Eisenmann as well as to Marilyn Todesco, Paula Smith-MacDonald, Libby Bixby and Beth Affanato. Kathryn Powell, Donald Scragg, Steve Harris and the scholars of the International Society of Anglo-Saxonists at the 1999 convention at the University of Notre Dame all made many corrections and useful suggestions. The King Alfred computer program was inspired by a suggestion from David I. Drout.

My student collaborators, David Dudek (who programmed the first version of King Alfred) and Rachel Kapelle (who found and parsed the sentences) not only contributed significantly to the project but also encouraged me to continue to work on it. Additional help came from Laura Kalafarski. Rebecca Epstein has significantly improved the book through her detailed criticism.

Wheaton's Library, Technology and Learning Committee partially funded the creation of the grammar with a generous stipend, and the original development of the King Alfred program was funded by a Gebbie student/faculty research grant. Jenny Lund encouraged me to begin work on the program. Mars faculty/student research stipends have supported the improvement and re-development of

King Alfred. I am grateful to Wheaton College for the continued support of this and other projects.

I want to especially thank Rachel Kapelle, Lisa Michaud and Bruce Gilchrist. Rachel selected and parsed many of the sample sentences. Lisa completely re-wrote the King Alfred program. As well as devising major innovations in the structure of the grammar, Bruce has written the appendix on sound changes. He has made significant improvements, fixing explanations, catching errors and expanding discussions. Scott Kleinman completely fixed the on-line version of the book and made many valuable suggestions.

Thanks also to Scott Nokes and Witan Publishing for believing in the value of the grammar.

My wife, Raquel M. D'Oyen, my daughter Rhys and my son Mitchell have generously allowed me the time and given me the inspiration to continue this work.

Finally, all of my students who have suffered through the various versions of King Alfred, King Alfred's Grammar and now Drout's Quick and Easy Old English (learning Anglo-Saxon on the way) in many ways wrote this book through their hard work and honest criticisms. I am grateful for all of their hard work and enthusiasm.

Michael D.C. Drout

Wheaton College and Dedham, Mass.

March 2012

INTRODUCTION

Old English, a term which is often used interchangeably with "Anglo-Saxon," is obviously no longer a spoken language. Because there are no living speakers of Old English to talk to, the techniques for teaching and learning Old English are somewhat different than those used for a living language. Although the goal of comprehending the target language remains the same, many of the approaches of conversational language instruction do not seem to work for Old English.

Rather than fluency in conversation, the main goal of any beginning Old English class needs to be acquiring the ability to translate and read the language. When you can translate Old English you will be able to read some of the very best poetry and most interesting prose that world literature has to offer. This grammar book and translation program are designed with the goal of giving a student the ability to translate as quickly as possible.

Translation ability has always been at the heart of Old English study, but the means by which this goal is reached are beginning to change. Old English has traditionally been taught the same ways as have Latin and Greek, but few students seem to be content with a purely analytical approach of memorizing paradigms and approaching the language as a logic puzzle. This resistance is unfortunate, because although Old English does not always unlock the treasures of its "word hoard" easily, the treasures therein are precious and the struggle to attain them is in itself a valuable effort.

But as Cnut, the great eleventh-century king, is supposed to have demonstrated, the tide does not stop coming in just because someone wants it to stop. The classical studies approach is clearly not working for all students of Old English.

Enter Drout's Quick and Easy Old English. It is our hope (borne out by a decade of testing in the classroom) that by helping students focus on problem areas and to spend more time learning things that aren't already known instead of repeating already mastered material, the process of learning Old English will be stripped of much of its drudgery. This grammar is structured to present material at the most basic, direct level possible. We have kept explanations as brief and straightforward as we can, and all key terms that are marked in bold are given definitions in the Glossary of Grammar Terms at the back of the book. At the back of the book students will also find a supplementary Appendix on Sound Changes. There is also an Old English Glossary (although this is not a good substitute for An Anglo-Saxon Dictionary by J. R. Clark-Hall) and a few pages of blank paradigm charts that can be printed out and used by students to learn declensions and conjugations more effectively. We hope all of these elements make Drout's Quick and Easy Old English useful to beginning Old English students of all backgrounds, not only to native English speakers, but also to students for whom Modern English is a second or third language.

Students who make a strong effort to master Old English grammar right from the beginning can almost always read Old English (with the help of a dictionary) by the end of the semester. By simplifying the language as much as possible, we hope we have enabled students to be free to pay more attention to the beauty and power of this oldest form of the language we speak today and (to steal King Alfred's words) to learn "those things that are most necessary for people to know."

1

A BRIEF HISTORY OF OLD ENGLISH

When the Anglo-Saxons first came to England from northern Germany in the fifth and sixth centuries, they brought their language with them. It is a Germanic language and has some fundamental similarities to modern German. If Anglo-Saxon had then developed undisturbed for several centuries we might have no more trouble reading an Old English text than we do reading something written by Chaucer at the end of the fourteenth century (students can start reading Chaucer with no special linguistic instruction, although they may need to go slowly and will probably require the help of footnotes for the first few weeks of a course). But political and cultural events changed the Anglo-Saxon language into the language we speak today.

The most important political influence upon the language was the Norman Conquest of 1066, when William the Conqueror, a prince of Normandy (a part of France), conquered England. William made French the language of the aristocracy and the law courts. Anglo-Norman French was an elite language, and the common people did not necessarily learn it as children, but it was the official language of the nation.

Over the next two centuries Anglo-Norman French mixed with Anglo-Saxon, probably because the children of the Norman-French aristocracy were being raised by servants who spoke Anglo-Saxon among themselves. What we call Middle English arose out of this language contact and earlier interactions between Old Norse and Anglo-Saxon. Middle English was less inflected than Anglo-Saxon, using the order of words in a sentence to indicate grammatical relationships, and the language absorbed much French vocabulary. Spoken between 1200 and 1400, Middle English is the language of Geoffrey Chaucer, William Langland, and the anonymous poet who wrote *Sir Gawain and the Green Knight*.

But as you can see by reading any brief passage from Chaucer, Chaucer's language is not our language. Around the year 1500, a linguistic event called "The Great Vowel Shift" occurred. No one really knows why, though there are many speculations, but within a generation or so the pronunciation of Middle English vowels was rearranged. For example, the "ee" sound in Chaucer's word "sweete" (pronounced to rhyme with "eight") became the "ee" sound in Modern English "sweet." Also the "i" in "April," which is Chaucer's time was pronounced to rhyme with Modern English "peel" became the short "i" sound in Modern English "April."

Once this vowel shift is complete, we have Early Modern English and, soon after, Modern English. Thus while Chaucer takes some getting used to, students can successfully read the writings of Shakespeare with very little formal instruction in his language. Our language, for all the new words added and changes in manners and style, is essentially the same as Shakespeare's. We could have understood Shakespeare, and he would have understood us, but he would not have understood the Anglo-Saxon writer Ælfric, and neither would Chaucer even though approximately the same amount of time separates Chaucer from Ælfric as separates Shakespeare from us.

Despite the differences between Old English and Modern English, the language retains a fundamental kinship to our own.

Students can thus expect to find learning Old English to be somewhat easier than learning a new "foreign" language such as Spanish or French. A semester's worth of hard work should be enough to give a student the ability to translate Old English poetry and prose. The key to success in this endeavor is to lay a solid foundation of grammatical understanding. While at first it may seem easy to "get the general idea" of a passage, if you take the time to figure out exactly how each word is working in a sentence you will find that the more complicated Old English sentences that we meet later in the semester will be less difficult to translate than they otherwise might be.

It is also important for students to realize that this short work is not a permanent substitute for an expansive, detailed grammar book, such as Mitchell and Robinson's *A Guide to Old English*. *Drout's Quick and Easy Old English* skips over exceptions to rules, complications of syntax and some subtleties of Old English grammar. The time in a semester is so short and the number of things worth learning so many that we feel justified in this simplification. Our purpose is to get students translating literature as quickly as humanly possible, thus preparing them for further study in Old English literature and culture.

2

OLD ENGLISH ORTHOGRAPHY

A few of the letters in Old English texts may be unfamiliar to you.

þ and Þ (thorn)   In Modern English we represent the sounds at the beginning of the word "the" and end of the word "with" with the digraph "th" (digraph is a term meaning two letters that used to represent one sound). Old English had two separate letters for the "th" sound. The first is written like this: þ. It is called thorn.

ð and Ð (eth)   Old English scribes could also represent the "th" sound with the letter ð (the capital letter version looks like a capital D with a short horizontal line: Ð). The letter is called eth, pronounced so that it rhymes with the first syllable in the word "feather."

Thorn and eth are used interchangeably to represent both voiced and unvoiced "th" sounds (the sound at the beginning of "there" is voiced; the sound at the end of "with" is unvoiced).

æ and Æ (ash)	This letter, called ash, may be familiar to you from old-fashioned spellings of words like "Encyclopædia." The digraph æ in Old English is pronounced the same way as the "a" in the words "bat" or "cat."

Below you will find some Modern English words with the "th" sound replaced by eth or thorn and some of the "a" sounds replaced with ash.

Ðat = That

ðousand = thousand

sixþ = sixth

þin = thin

wiðer = wither

bæckground = background

Æppetite = Appetite

Æt = At

hæmmer = hammer

Æcknowledge = Acknowledge

Note:

In addition to *thorn, eth,* and *ash,* there are a few additional letters used in Anglo-Saxon manuscripts that are unfamiliar to Modern English speakers. The letter 3, called **yogh**, is pronounced like Modern English "y" or "g" depending upon the word in which it is found. *Yogh* (the name is pronounced so that it rhymes with the Scottish word "loch") is the antecedent of the Modern English word "yoke."

A letter which looks like Modern English "p," called **wynn**, (which comes from a **rune** by that name) is pronounced like Modern English "w."

"Tyronian Note," which looks somewhat like a number seven (ꝺ), is a common medieval abbreviation for "and." Tyronian Note is used in some editions of Old English texts, but editors normally expand it to *and* or *ond*.

Although *yogh* and *wynn* are found in Old English manuscripts, most editors replace them with their Modern English equivalents while they leave *thorn, eth,* and *ash* in place. The reasons for this inconsistency are bound up in the early history of Anglo-Saxon studies and the preferences of the editors who made the first print editions. If you decide to learn about **paleography**, the study of ancient writing, or work directly with Anglo-Saxon **manuscripts** or **facsimiles**, you will have to learn to recognize *yogh, wynn* and also special forms of the letters "s," "r," and "f." But most Old English texts are edited so that the only unfamiliar letters printed are *thorn, eth,* and *ash*: þ, ð, æ).

3

OLD ENGLISH PRONUNCIATION

Old English is a "dead" language. No one, not even the children of the most fanatical Anglo-Saxonists (although some of us are working on it) grows up speaking Anglo-Saxon as a cradle tongue. But it is nevertheless worth learning to pronounce the language, and not only so you can impress people at cocktail parties. Reading Old English words and paradigms aloud can help many students to memorize important information more easily. Also, Old English poetry evolved as an oral medium: although written texts are all that remain of Old English poetry, scholars have deduced that the Anglo-Saxons preferred to have their poetry presented orally. Finally, Old English poetry is particularly beautiful when read aloud.

Vowels

There are many relatively complicated charts that explain the pronunciation of Old English vowels, but the power of new information technology has suggested to us a better way to learn how to pronounce Old English words: You can log into *Drout's Quick and Easy Old English* (or the older *King Alfred's Grammar*) on the web and simply click on the hyperlinks to hear the word in Old English.

Most editors use **macrons** (a horizontal bar over the top of a vowel) to indicate vowel length. A **long vowel** is indicated by a macron; a **short vowel** is one without a macron. Macrons to indicate vowel length do not appear in Anglo-Saxon manuscripts.

o short **a** is pronounced like the Modern English "o" sound in "contact."

o long **ā** is pronounced like the "a" sound in Modern English "father."

o short **æ** is pronounced like the "a" sound in Modern English "cat" or "bat."

o long **ǣ** is pronounced like the "a" sound in Modern English "band"

o short **e** is pronounced like the "e" sound in Modern English "bet."

o long **ē** is pronounced to rhyme with Modern English "way."

o short **i** is pronounced like the "i" sound in Modern English "his."

o long **ī** is pronounced like the "i" sound in Modern English "machine."

o short **o** is pronounced like the "o" sound in Modern English "pond."

o long **ō** is pronounced like the "o" sound in Modern English "go."

o short **u** is pronounced like the "u" sound in Modern English "bull."

- long **ū** is pronounced like the "oo" sound in Modern English "school."

- short **y** is pronounced like the "i" sound in Modern English "will."

- long **ȳ** is pronounced like the "oo" sound in Modern English "school," but with the lips slightly pursed.

Diphthongs

Diphthongs are combinations of two vowels. Modern English diphthongs include such combinations as the "ea" in "beast," the "ie" in "convenient," and the "ei" in "weight." Explanations of pronunciation of Old English diphthongs are notoriously confusing, so we'll simply rely on demonstrating the pronunciation of representative words.

- short **e** + **a** is pronounced like the "ai" sound in "fail."

- long **ē** + **a** is pronounced like the "a" sound in "favor."

- short **i** + **e** is pronounced like "ie" sound in "yield."

- long **ī** + **e** is pronounced like the "ea" sound in "beard."

- short **e** + **o** is pronounced so that the "e" sounds like the "ai" sound in "air" and the "o" sounds like the "oa"

- in "oar." *Eorþan* is pronounced "ay-oar-than."

- long **ē** + **o** is pronounced so that the "e" has the sound of the "a" in "favor" and the "o" has the sound of the "oa" in "boat": *Beowulf* is pronounced "Bay-oh-wolf."

Front vowels and back vowels: vowels can be classified by the different places in the mouth in which they are pronounced. For example, if you say "flee," you will feel vibration in the front part of your mouth. This is an example of a **front vowel**. If you say "cut," you will feel vibration in the back part of your mouth. This is an example of a **back vowel**. Front vowels in Old English include *e* and *i*. Back vowels include *a, o* and *u*. The difference between front vowels and back vowels is significant because the vowel that follows a *g* or a *c* in Old English determines how that consonant is pronounced (see below).

Consonants

Most Old English consonants are pronounced the same way as their Modern English equivalents. We give the exceptions below.

c can be pronounced either as a hard "c" sound, represented in Modern English by "k," or as the sound that is represented in Modern English by "ch." If *c* precedes a **front vowel**, it is pronounced like "ch": *ceosan* is pronounced "chay-oh-san." If *c* precedes a **back vowel**, it is pronounced like "k": *cuman* is pronounced "koo-man." Some editors indicate the "ch" pronunciation of *c* by putting a dot above the consonant (ċ).

f is usually pronounced as it is in Modern English. However, when it is in **intervocalic** position (between two vowels), it is pronounced with a **voiced** sound and so like Modern English "v." Thus *heofan* is pronounced "hay-oh-van."

g can also be pronounced two ways. Before **front vowels** ("i" and "e") it is pronounced like the Modern English "y" in the word "yes": *gifu* is pronounced "yif-u" (this pronunciation is called **palatal g**). When "g" is used before **back vowels** ("a," "0," and "u") it is pronounced the same as Modern English "g" in "golden": *gōda* ("go-da") (this pronunciation is called **velar g**). Some editors indicate this voiced pronunciation of "g" by putting a dot above the consonant.

h is never silent. It is pronounced with a bit of a throat-clearing sound, like the "ch" at the end of Scottish "loch" or German "Bach." "h" is also used in combination with the "semi-vowels" (also called "liquids") "r," "l," and "w" in ways not familiar in Modern English: *hlaford, hronræd, hwæt.*

r is trilled or rolled as it is in British English or Russian.

sc is pronounced like Modern English "sh": *scip* ("ship")

Vowel changes from Old English to Modern English

As Old English evolved to Middle and then Modern English, vowels changed in words in a consistent way (see the Appendix on Sound Changes for a detailed discussion). These changes can help you to translate Anglo-Saxon words even if you have not yet looked them up in the dictionary and memorized their meanings.

We suggest learning that vowel relationships in both directions, from OE to ModE and from ModE to OE That is, learn that a⇒o and also that o⇐a (a evolves to o and o is derived from a).

a ⇒ o

The Anglo-Saxon long **a**, which was pronounced like the sound in "baa" (i.e., a sheep call), changed in Modern English into the "o" sound in "boat."

- la = lo!

- wa = woe

- na = no

- ga = go

- da = doe

- ta = toe
- swa = so
- hwa = who
- twa = two
- hal = whole
- mal = mole
- þrawan = to throw
- sawan = to sow
- mawan = to mow
- crawan = to crow
- cnawan = to know
- ham = home
- lam = loam
- fam = foam
- ac = oak
- stracian = stroke
- spaca = spoke
- rad = road
- gad = goad
- tad = toad
- abad = abode

- o wrat = wrote

- o gat = goat

- o bat = boat

- o rap = rope

- o sape = soap

- o grapian = grope

- o Papa = Pope

(These changes explain why we say "Pope" but "Papacy" and "Papal.": "Papa" comes from Latin "father" and was borrowed into English early enough to undergo the vowel change. "Papacy" and "Papal" were borrowed later and didn't go through the shift.)

e ⇒ ee

The Anglo-Saxon Long **e**, which was pronounced like Modern English "ay", turned into Modern English **e**, pronounced as the sound in "beef"

- o he = he

- o ðe = thee

- o we = we

- o me = me

- o hedan = to heed

- o redan = to read

- o steda = steed

- o sped = speed

- o fedan = feed

- o ned = need

- o bredan = to breed

- o bledan = to bleed

- o creda = creed

- o swete = sweet

- o scet = sheet

- o fet = feet

- o metan = meet

- o gretan = greet

- o bete = beet

- o wepan = to weep

i ⇒ i

The Anglo-Saxon **i** was pronounced like the ee in "beet." It evolves into the Modern English **i**, pronounced as in the words "iron," "I" or "eye"

- o hwil = while

- o mil = mile

- o liðe = lithe

- o wriðan = to writhe

- o bliðe = blithe

- risan = to rise

- wis = wise

- cnif = knife

- wif = wife

- drifan = to drive

- fif-e = five

- ðin = thine

- swin = swine

- scinan = to shine

- win = wine

- rim = rime ("now almost invariably spelt rhyme, by a needless and ignorant confusion with the unrelated word rhythm, which is of Greek origin, whereas rime is purely English" says the Reverend Walter W. Skeat)

- lic = like

- strican = to strike

- dic = dike

- idel = idel

- ridan = to ride

- side = side

- slidan = slide

- wid = wide

- o glidan = to glide
- o cidan = to chide
- o tid = tide
- o bidan = bide
- o bridel = bridel
- o smitan = smite
- o writan = write
- o hwit = white
- o bitan = bite

o ⇒ oo

Anglo-Saxon long **o** was pronounced like the **oa** in Modern English "boat." It becomes, in Modern English, the "oo" sound in "blue" or "goose"

- o sco = shoe
- o do = do
- o to = to
- o stol = stool
- o col = cool
- o tol = tool
- o soð = sooth
- o toð = tooth

- o   gos = goose

- o   non = noon

- o   hof = hoof

- o   spon = spoon

- o   glom = gloom

- o   brom = broom

- o   dom = doom

- o   foda = food

- o   mod = mood

u ⇒ ow

The Anglo-Saxon long **u** was pronounced like the "u" in "mule." It becomes pronounced like the Modern English sound marked by "ow" in "cow" and "vow."

- o   hu = how

- o   ðu = thou

- o   nu = now

- o   cu = cow

- o   bru = brow

- o   ure = our

- o   sur = sour

- o   scur = shower

- bur = bower
- ule = owl
- ful = fowl
- suð = south
- muð = mouth
- hus = house
- lus = louse
- mus = mouse
- þusand = thousand
- dun = down
- tun = town
- brun = brown

y ⇒ i

The sound of the Anglo-Saxon long **y** is like the sound in "boot" but made with the lips slightly pursed.

- hyr = hire
- fyr = fire
- lys = lice
- mys = mice
- hyd = hide (skin)
- hydan = to hide

o   bryd = bride

o   pryte = pride

æ ⇒ a

The sound of Anglo-Saxon ash is that of the **a** in "cat" of "bat." It becomes the sound represented by the **ee** in "beet."

o   sæ = sea

o   fær = fear

o   ræran = to rear

o   æl = eel

o   mæl = meal

o   hælan = to heal

o   dælan = to deal

o   hæþ = heath

o   hæðen = heathen

o   scæþ = sheath

o   wræþ = wreath

o   tæsan = to tease

o   læfan = to leave

o   clæne = clean

o   mænan = to mean

o   læce = leech

- o spræc = speech

- o rǣcan = to reach

- o tǣcan = to teach

- o blǣcan = to bleach

- o wǣd = weed (meaning clothes; "widow's weeds")

- o sǣd = seed

- o grǣdig = greedy

- o dǣd = deed

- o rǣdan = to read

- o lǣdan = to lead

- o nǣdl = needle

- o stǣt = street

- o blǣtan = to bleat

- o hǣto = heat

- o hwǣte = wheat

- o slǣp = sleep

The addition of a **g** (vocalic or velar **g**, pronounced as Modern English **y**) after long æ produces a diphthong that would be pronounced to rhyme with "eye":

- o grǣg = gray

- o clǣg = clay

4

GRAMMAR CONCEPTS: PARTS OF SPEECH

We want to get right into translating and reading Old English sentences, but first we need to review a few basic grammatical concepts. Since no one speaks Old English as a native language (although some scholars are so good with it that they come close; J.R.R. Tolkien composed poetry in Old English), we can't use many of the conversational approaches used to teach modern languages. Old English is thus taught the way Latin was taught for centuries: as a "dead" language, one that people read more than they speak. This grammar book attempts to make such an approach easier and more exciting than earlier methods of teaching, but in the end there is a significant amount of memorization you need to do in order to understand the texts. Memorization of vocabulary words is necessary for learning all languages, but to understand Old English a student needs to learn to recognize certain grammatical concepts. Although using "it just feels right" can be a perfectly acceptable approach to learning the grammar of a living, spoken language, it simply isn't a powerful enough tool for learning Old English. We need some terms to talk about grammar.

We begin with a review of the **parts of speech**. Every word in a language can be put into one or more categories that explain how that word is used. Knowing what part of speech a word is will help you to translate Old English. There are, for our purposes in this simplified grammar book, seven parts of speech that you need to be able to recognize.

Nouns: "A noun is a person, place or thing" is a rough definition of nouns. Nouns are naming words. "King," "Alfred," "crown," "kingdom" and "power" are all nouns.

Verbs: "Verb: that's what's happening." Verbs are action words. "Ruled," "wears," "carries," "to wander" and "fought" are all verbs.

Pronouns: Pronouns are used in place of nouns. "He," "she," "it," "who," "whom," "that," "which," "we," "they" and "us" are all pronouns. This grammar book groups words like "this," "that," "these" and "those," as well as "a," "an" and "the," with the pronouns and calls these words **demonstrative** pronouns, although grammarians would probably call some of them **articles**, and linguists would identify them as **determiners**.

Adjectives: Adjectives are words used to describe nouns. "Royal," "golden," "lofty," "powerful," "hardy" and "strong" are all adjectives.

Adverbs: Adverbs are words used to describe verbs or adjectives. "Slowly," "steadily," "angrily," "powerfully" and "very" are all adverbs. Words that indicate time, such as "then," "when," "later" and "before," are also adverbs.

Prepositions: Prepositions are short explanatory words that indicate things such as location, direction and possession: "with," "to," "under," "over," "by" and "for" are all prepositions.

Conjunctions: Conjunctions are connecting words: "and," "but," "or" and "nor" are all conjunctions.

Some exercises to practice recognizing the parts of speech

Label each part of speech in the sentences below.

Parts of speech: noun, pronoun, verb, adjective, adverb, preposition, conjunction. Mark articles as demonstrative pronouns.

1. The king ruled the great kingdom for a long time.

2. The battle was fought at the thorn tree.

3. Alfred struggled against the rapacious Vikings.

4. Many monks traveled to the ruined city.

5. Alfred's warriors fought fiercely against the evil invaders.

6. The king spread learning and culture through the land.

7. Some historians say Alfred is the first true king of England.

8. With effort and hard work, Alfred learned to read difficult Latin books.

9. Alfred's father made the long journey to Rome and returned quickly.

10. The Alfred jewel may have been created for Alfred.

5

GRAMMAR CONCEPTS: WORD FUNCTIONS

Now that you've re-familiarized yourself with the various parts of speech, we need to discuss the ways in which these parts can be arranged to make meaningful sentences.

When we speak or write, we don't just put the words down on the page at random:

dog cat the the towards ran quickly brown black.

We organize them in certain ways to convey meaning:

The brown dog ran quickly towards the black cat.

Or

The brown cat ran towards the dog quickly.

The rules by which we arrange words to convey meaning are called **syntax**.

Different words, depending on where they are in the sentence, or which endings we attach to them, perform different functions in a sentence. Simplified for the purpose of this grammar, these functions are:

Subjects:

The subject is the "doer" or "actor." In the sentence "<u>Alfred</u> ate the cakes," <u>Alfred</u> is the subject. Nouns and pronouns are used for subjects.

Verbs:

The verb is the action being done. In the sentence "Alfred <u>ate</u> the cakes," "<u>ate</u>" is the verb.

Direct Objects

The direct object is the receiver of the action. In the sentence "Alfred ate the <u>cakes</u>," "<u>cakes</u>" is the direct object.

Indirect Objects:

The indirect object is the secondary receiver of the action. In the sentence "Alfred carried the sword to the <u>battle</u>," "<u>battle</u>" is the indirect object (and "sword," which is receiving the action, is the direct object). Indirect objects are often called "objects of prepositions" because in Modern English we use prepositions to indicate the sort of action being secondarily received: in the phrases "to the <u>battle</u>," "with the <u>sword</u>," "under the thorn <u>tree</u>," "by the <u>river</u>," "<u>battle</u>," "<u>sword</u>," "<u>tree</u>" and "<u>river</u>" are the objects of their respective prepositions.

Modifiers:

Modifiers describe subjects, verbs and objects. In the sentence "With his <u>old</u> sword, Alfred <u>quickly</u> killed the Viking," "<u>old</u>" is an adjective that modifies "sword" (it describes the condition of the sword), and "quickly" is an adverb that modifies "killed" (it explains how the killing was done). Adjectives describe subjects and objects; adverbs describe verbs and adjectives.

In Old English certain pronouns (**demonstratives**) are used as modifiers: In the sentence "this sword belongs to that man," "this" describes the sword and "that" describes the man. Likewise "a," "an," and "the," which we call **articles** in Modern English, are, in Old English grammar, special pronouns (demonstratives) that are used as modifiers: "The sword" is different from "a sword" because the modifiers "the" and "a" are providing different descriptions.

Genitives are an important sub-set of modifiers in Old English. Genitives are possessives: they indicate ownership. A noun with a genitive ending, like the Modern English apostrophe-s ('s), is used as an adjective to modify another noun. In the sentence "Alfred's sword was old," "Alfred's" is a genitive: a noun (Alfred) has had the genitive ending ('s) added to it. A good rule of thumb for dealing with the genitive is to translate it as "of X" where "X" is the noun that has the genitive ending. Thus "Alfred's sword" could be translated as "the sword of Alfred."

Function Words:

What we are calling "function words" are prepositions and conjunctions that don't mean anything in themselves but serve to indicate the ways other words relate to each other. Prepositions indicate relationships and conjunctions join things together. In the sentences "Alfred fought with the Vikings and won the battle by the thorn tree," "with" and "by" are prepositions that indicate relationships (where the battle was fought and whom it was fought against) and "and" indicates that two parts of the sentence are joined together.

The above description of word functions is radically simplified, but it should be enough to explain the concepts in the grammar and get you translating Old English as soon as possible. The important point to remember is that we will need to use certain orders of words or put certain endings on words in order to indicate what roles they are playing in a sentence. We will go over these concepts in more detail in the following sections.

Some exercises to practice recognizing word functions.

Label the subjects, verbs and direct objects in the sentences below.

1. Alfred killed the Viking.

2. The ruler of the West Saxons sent a message.

3. Guthorm attacked the English king.

4. The herald struck his shield and spoke.

5. The warriors dropped their swords.

Label the subjects, verbs, direct objects and indirect objects / objects of prepositions in the following sentences.

1. Alfred killed the Viking with his sword.

2. The ruler of the West Saxons sent a message to Guthorm.

3. Guthorm negotiated with the English king about the treaty.

4. The herald struck his shield and inspired the warriors.

5. The warriors dropped their swords on the ground.

Label the subjects, verbs, direct objects, indirect objects / objects of prepositions, and modifiers in the following sentences.

1. Alfred killed the vicious Viking with his old sword.

2. The kind ruler sent a message to brave Guthorm.

3. Wise Guthorm negotiated with the trustworthy English king about the important treaty.

4. The grizzled herald struck his linden shield and loudly inspired the tired warriors.

5. The hungry warriors quickly dropped their notched swords onto the wet ground.

6

GRAMMAR CONCEPTS:
WORD ORDER AND CASES

Now that you have made yourself familiar with the parts of speech and the ways different types of words function in a sentence to make meaning, we are ready to move on to Old English itself.

Modern English is what is called an **analytic language**. For the most part, it uses the order of words in a sentence to indicate grammatical and logical relationships. Thus

The <u>dog</u> ate the *cat*

means something very different from

The <u>cat</u> ate the *dog*.

Both sentences are made up of exactly the same words, but they mean totally different things. Why? Because we have used the arrangement of words in the sentence to specify which word is the <u>subject</u> and which is the *direct object*.

In the first example, we know that "dog" is the subject of the sentence because it comes before the verb. Likewise, we know that "cat" is the object of the sentence (it receives the action) because it comes after the verb ("ate").

Things didn't work exactly this way in Old English. Old English (like Latin, Greek, Russian and many other languages) is an **inflected language**. Instead of relying on word order to indicate relationships, Old English attaches endings to each word to indicate relationships. These endings are called **inflections**.

Different endings mark words as subjects (the thing performing an action), direct objects (things directly receiving the action), indirect objects (things indirectly receiving the action), objects of prepositions, and genitives (things possessed by other things).

(If you aren't sure you completely understand these different word functions, go back to the previous chapter and look over the explanations).

Because word endings rather than word order indicate grammatical relationships, word order is not nearly as important in Old English as it is in Modern English. Therefore words in an Old English sentence can be arranged in various ways without changing the meaning of a sentence. There are of course some limits to this flexibility. The study of these rules and regularities is the field of Old English **syntax**. In general, syntax in poetry is more flexible than syntax in prose.

Thus, in Old English

Dog+(subject ending) ate cat+(direct object ending).

means exactly the same thing as:

Cat+(object ending) ate dog+(subject ending).

and also the same thing as:

Ate dog+(subject ending) *cat+(object ending)*.

On the other hand,

    Dog+(object ending) ate cat+(subject ending).

means something entirely different.

Don't panic: we do in fact use endings in Modern English to indicate grammatical function (think of "s", "-ing", "-tion", "-ly", "-y" and others).

To understand Old English, you do not need to learn (very much) about word order. You do, however, need to learn your endings and their grammatical functions.

Some exercises to practice using endings to determine the sense of a sentence.

"Translate" the sentences below into correct Modern English word order.

1. *Vikings (direct object)* Alfred (subject) fought against

2. gave **to the king (indirect object)** the monks (subject) *the jewel (direct object)*

3. Wulfgar (subject) **to Alfred (indirect object)** pledged *his support (direct object)*

4. English warriors (subject) *many Viking ships (direct object)* burned

5. Ate crows (subject) *many bodies (direct object)*

Cases

Endings for nouns, pronouns and adjectives in Old English are divided into five categories of grammatical function called **cases**. A list and brief description is given below.

Nominative: The naming case, the nominative is used for **subjects** and for **predicate nominatives** (words that rename the subject of the sentence).

Genitive: The possession case, the genitive is used to indicate ownership.

Accusative: The direct object case, the accusative is used to indicate direct receivers of an action. The accusative case also indicates "motion towards," can be the object of the preposition such as "to," and can indicate the passage of time.

Dative / The indirect object and prepositional case, the
Instrumental: dative/instrumental is used to indicate indirect receivers of action and objects of prepositions. The dative is also used to indicate locations of non-moving objects (**locative dative**) and the instrumental identifies things that are being used (instruments).

A list of all the possible endings for a word is called a **declension**. In Old English, nouns, pronouns and adjectives are all **declined**; that is, they change their endings based upon their grammatical function (or the grammatical function of the words they modify) in the sentence.

We use cases in Modern English when we use "he" or "she" as the subject of a sentence but "him" or "her" as the direct object (similarly, "who" for subjects and "whom" for objects). In Old

English, cases are used more consistently and logically than in Modern English.

The Nominative Case

The nominative is the naming case, used for the **subject** of the sentence.

Nominative nouns can be **singular**:

Alfred is my name.

"Alfred" is the subject of the sentence, so "Alfred" would be in the nominative.

Nominative nouns can also be **plural**:

The brothers divided the kingdom.

o   "Brothers" is the subject of the sentence, so "brothers" would be in the nominative case.

o   In Old English, **nouns**, **pronouns** and **adjectives** can all take the nominative case.

o   If a noun is in the nominative, the pronouns and adjectives grammatically related to that noun will also be in the nominative. This principle is called **case agreement** among nouns, pronouns and adjectives.

That great king ruled the kingdom.

"King" is the **subject** of the sentence, so it is in the nominative. "That" and "great" describe "king", so they are also in the nominative.

Having "that" and "great" in the nominative as well as "king" is an example of **case agreement** among adjectives, pronouns and nouns.

> **Note:** Dictionaries and glossaries list nouns and adjectives in their **nominative** forms.

The Genitive Case

The genitive is the case for possession, used to indicate that one thing is owned by, controlled by, connected to or a part of another.

In Modern English we usually indicate genitives by using apostrophe-s ('s) or the preposition "of".

Alfred's kingdom was famous.

or:

The kingdom of Alfred was famous.

The kingdom is the subject of the sentence and is in the nominative case. Because the kingdom belongs to Alfred, "Alfred" is in the genitive case (the ownership / possession case).

Genitives can be **singular** (as above) or **plural**:

The swords of the men were sharp.

This sentence can also be phrased:

The men's swords were sharp.

In Old English, adjectives and pronouns may also take the genitive case:

His sword was sharp.

(or, The sword of him was sharp.)

The power of that large kingdom was great.

- o "Sword" and "power" are the subjects of the sentences, so they are in the nominative case.

- o "His" is a genitive pronoun referring to the sword.

- o "Of that large kingdom" is a phrase composed of a demonstrative pronoun ("that"), an adjective ("large") and a noun ("kingdom"), all in the genitive and all of which refer to the word "power."

- o Having "that," "large" and "kingdom" in the genitive case is an example of **case agreement** among nouns, demonstratives and adjectives.

The Accusative Case

The accusative is the **direct object** case. It is used to indicate the receiver of an action.

Alfred praised *Wulfstan.*

The accusative can be **singular** (as above) or **plural**:

Alfred rewarded the *warriors.*

- o Alfred is the subject of the sentences because he performs the action.

- o "Wulfstan" and "the warriors" are the direct objects of the sentences because they receive the action.

In Old English, adjectives and pronouns may also take the accusative case:

Alfred rewarded *those brave warriors.*

- o Alfred is the subject of the sentence because he is performing the action.

- o The "warriors" are the direct object of the sentence because they are receiving the action (the reward).

- o "Those" is a demonstrative pronoun that refers to the warriors, so it is in the accusative case.

- o "Brave" is an adjective that, because it refers to the warriors (who are receiving the action), is also in the accusative case.

- o Having "those" and "brave" in the accusative as well as "warriors" is an example of **case agreement** among adjectives, pronouns and nouns.

The accusative case can also be used to indicate "motion towards" something.

The Viking ships came *into the harbor*.

The Viking ships are moving *towards* the harbor, so the entire phrase "into the harbor" is in the **accusative** case.

If the ships were *staying* in the harbor, the phrase "in the harbor" would be in the **dative** case.

The Dative and Instrumental Cases

The Dative Case

The dative case can be used for both **indirect objects** and **objects of prepositions**.

Dative for Indirect Objects

The dative is the indirect object case, used to indicate the secondary receiver of an action.

Alfred praised Wulfstan to <u>Edward</u>.

The dative can be singular (as above) or plural:

Alfred praised Wulfstan to <u>the warriors.</u>

- o Alfred is the subject of the sentences because he is performing the action.

- o "Wulfstan" is the direct object of the sentence because he is receiving the action.

- o "Edward" and "the warriors" are the indirect objects because they secondarily receive the action.

In Old English, adjectives and pronouns can also take the dative case:

Alfred praised Wulfstan to <u>those brave warriors</u>.

- Alfred is the subject of the sentence because he is performing the action.

- "Wulfstan" is the direct object of the sentence because he is receiving the action.

- "Wulfstan" would be in the accusative case.

- "Warriors" are the indirect objects because they secondarily receive the action.

- "Those warriors" would be in the dative case.

- "Those" is a demonstrative pronoun that refers to the warriors, so it is in the dative case.

- "Brave" is an adjective that, because it refers to the warriors (who are secondarily receiving the action), is also in the dative case.

- Having "those" and "brave" in the dative as well as "warriors" is an example of **case agreement** among adjectives, pronouns and nouns.

Dative with Prepositions

In Old English the objects of most **prepositions** take the dative case ("of," which can take the **genitive**, and "to," which can take the **accusative**, are the more common exceptions).

Alfred struggled with <u>illness</u>.

Alfred hid in <u>Æthelny</u>. (Alfred is not moving, so the case is dative rather than accusative)

Alfred prayed for <u>victory</u>.

- o "Alfred" is the subject of each sentence because he is performing the actions.

- o "Illness," "Æthelny" and "victory" are the objects of the prepositions "with," "by" and "for," so they are in the dative case.

In Old English, adjectives and pronouns also can take the dative case if they are linked to the object of a preposition.

Alfred struggled with <u>that horrible illness.</u>

- o Alfred is the subject of the sentence because he is performing the action.

- o "Illness" is the object of the preposition "with," so it is in the dative case.

- o "That" is a demonstrative pronoun that refers to "illness," so it is in dative case.

- o "Horrible" is an adjective that refers to "illness," so it is in the dative case.

- o Having "that" and "horrible" in the dative case as well as "illness" is an example of **case agreement** among adjectives, nouns and pronouns.

The Instrumental Case

Even though many books of Old English grammar separate the **dative** and **instrumental** cases, it is easier to think of the instrumental as just another use of the dative (the endings are the same for nouns; some pronouns have different instrumental forms).

An instrumental noun is one that is used to accomplish something as the instrument of the action (the instrumental case is roughly comparable to the ablative case in Latin).

In Old English instrumentals can be recognized as nouns in the dative case that are not **indirect objects** and aren't preceded by a preposition.

Alfred killed the Viking with a sword.

"Sword" is in the instrumental case because it is the instrument Alfred used to kill the Viking. However, it is just as easy to think of "sword" being the object of "with," and thus in the dative.

Old English gives a writer the option of leaving out "with" and simply saying

Alfred killed a Viking sword(+dative ending).

(note that "sword" is in the dative / instrumental case)

This sentence could be rephrased:

Alfred killed a Viking by means of a sword.

In Old English, adjectives and pronouns also can take the instrumental case if they are linked to an instrumental noun (or, if they are stand-alone pronouns, if they are being used as an instrument).

Alfred killed the Viking with <u>that trusty sword</u>.

- o "Alfred" is the subject of the sentence because he is performing the action.

- o "sword" is the means by which the action was accomplished, so it is in the instrumental case.

- o "that" is a demonstrative pronoun that refers to "sword," so it is in instrumental case.

- o "trusty" is an adjective that refers to "sword," so it is in the instrumental case.

- o Having "that" and "trusty" in the instrumental case as well as "sword" is an example of **case agreement** among adjectives, nouns and pronouns.

Quick Review of Cases

The endings on a word indicate which case it belongs to. In turn, the case indicates what function the word is performing in the sentence, whether it is the subject (nominative), the direct object (accusative), the indirect object or object of a preposition (dative), or if it is a possessive (genitive) form.

Some exercises for identifying cases.

Label each word in the sentences below with its appropriate case, nominative, genitive, accusative, dative or instrumental. Remember that verbs, adverbs and prepositions do not need to be identified with a case.

1. Few kings rule large kingdoms well.

2. One great king ruled England.

3. Skilled smiths made Alfred's sword.

4. The warrior struck the Viking with the heavy axe.

5. Alfred gave the jewel to the bishop.

6. Before the king arrived in Athelney, he had many adventures.

7. Many fierce Vikings invaded England after the eighth century.

8. Some brave warriors and desperate families fought the invaders.

9. The swords of the Vikings were stained with the blood of the monks.

10. Scholars worked hard to rebuild the culture of England.

PERSONAL PRONOUNS

Now that we've reviewed basic grammatical concepts we can finally move on to translating actual Old English sentences.

We'll begin with personal pronouns. Since we can find many simple sentences that use them, and since they are so common, it makes sense to memorize them right away.

In Modern English the personal pronouns include: "I," "you," "he," "she," "it," "we," "they," "them," "us," "him," "her."

Personal pronouns are used in statements and commands, but not in questions; **interrogative pronouns** (like "who," "whom," "what") are used there.

There are three persons for pronouns in Old English (**first person** = speaker; **second person** = person being addressed; **third person** = third person being spoken about). The third person has **masculine, neuter** and **feminine** forms.

Like Modern English, Old English has both **singular** and **plural** forms for the personal pronouns. But Old English also has a **dual** form, used to indicate two closely associated persons-two people working or fighting together, husband and wife, or lovers.

Remember that the **case** of a pronoun indicates how it functions grammatically in a sentence. Nominatives are subjects, genitives are possessive modifiers, accusatives are direct objects, and datives are objects of prepositions and indirect objects.

Paradigms: A paradigm is simply a list of all the possible grammatical forms of a word. It is usually arranged in a table, so that you can easily look up the forms that you need to translate. It's essential that you memorize your Old English paradigms so that you don't have to waste precious time flipping through your grammar book but can instead focus on translating.

Study tip: You can either memorize the paradigm visually, by creating a blank paradigm and filling in the boxes with the words you've memorized (this is the method that most students use for Old English), or, if you are a more aural learner, you can recite the paradigm so that you can memorize it. The most successful students often combine both of these methods. There are blank paradigms at the back of this grammar book. You can also download and print blank paradigms from the website.

First Person Personal Pronouns Paradigm

Case	Singular	Dual	Plural
Nominative	**ic** = I	**wit** = we two	**wē** = we
Genitive	**mīn** = mine	**uncer** = of us two (of ours)	**ūser** or **ūre** = of us, our
Accusative	**mē** or **mec** = me (direct object)	**unc** or **uncit** = us two (direct object)	**ūs** or **ūsic** = us (direct object)
Dative / Instrumental	**mē** = with me (or indirect object)	**unc** = with us two (or indirect object)	**ūs** = with us (or indirect object)

Note how familiar the singular and plural forms are. These forms have been conserved almost without change from Old English to Modern English. They also demonstrate that **cases** still exist in Modern English (for example, we use "I" as a subject but "me" as an object).

Second Person Personal Pronouns Paradigm

Case	Singular	Dual	Plural
Nominative	**þē** = you (singular)	**git** = you two	**gē** = you (plural: "y'all" or "younz")
Genitive	**þīn** = your [thine] (singular)	**incer** = of your two (yours)	**ēower** = your (plural: "y'all's" or "younz's")
Accusative	**þ ē** or **þec** = you (direct object)	**inc** or **incit** = you two (direct object)	**ēow** or **ēowic** = you (plural direct object)
Dative / Instrumental	**þē** = with you (or indirect object)	**inc** = with you two (or indirect object)	**ēow** = with you (or indirect object)

Third Person Personal Pronouns Paradigm

Case	Masculine	Neuter	Feminine	All Genders Plural
Nominative	**hē** = he	**hit** = it	**hēo** or **hīo** = she	**hī** or **hīe** = they
Genitive	**his** =his	**his** = its	**hire** = hers	**hira** = theirs
Accusative	**hine** = him (direct object)	**hit** = it (direct object)	**hī** or **hīe** = her (direct object)	**hī** or **hīe** = them (direct object)
Dative / Instrumental	**him** = with him (indirect object)	**him** = with it (indirect object)	**hire** =with her (indirect object)	**him** or **heom** = with them (indirect object)

> **Note**: The genitive pronouns can be used adjectivally (i.e., as **possessive adjectives**), in which case they are **declined** the same way an adjective is. We will return to this point in Chapter 11.

Interrogative Pronouns

Interrogative Pronouns are "question words": "who" and "what."

Who was the king of the West Saxons?

"Who" is the subject of the sentence. An interrogative pronoun stands in for what would be a personal pronoun if the sentence were a statement. Thus in this case, "who" could replace "he" if the question were answered: "He was the king of the West Saxons."

> **Note**: Interrogative pronouns have *five* (rather than four) case forms. The instrumental case is here different from the dative.

There are masculine and neuter forms. Masculine interrogative pronouns are used for both masculine and feminine nouns.

Interrogative Pronouns Paradigm

Case	Masculine	Neuter
Nominative	**hwā** = who	**hwæt** = what
Genitive	**hwæs** = of who (whose)	**hwæs** = of who (whose)
Accusative	**hwone** = whom (direct object)	**hwæt** = what (direct object)
Dative	**hwǣm** or **hwām** = with whom (or indirect object)	**hwǣm** or **hwām** = with whom (or indirect object)
Instrumental	**hwī** or **hwon** = by means of whom	**hwī** or **hwon** = by means of what

Note that neuter forms are the same in the nominative and the accusative cases, just as they are in Latin.

Chapter 7 Vocabulary

Note: Learn these words *in addition* to memorizing the personal pronouns.

Nouns

gryþ	quarter, truce	(accusative)
heofonas	the heavens	(plural of *heofon*; accusative)
īse	ice	(dative)
kyng	king	(nominative)
mann	man	(nominative)
Olāfe	Olaf	(proper name; dative)

Verbs

āstah	ascended	(past 1st and 3rd person singular of *āstīgan*)
cōmon	came	(past plural of *cuman*)
fēoll	fell	(past 1st and 3rd person singular of *[ge]feallan*)
geaf	gave	(past 1st and 3rd singular of *giefan*)
gebēte	repented	(past 1st and 3rd singular of *[ge]bētan*)
slæpð	sleeps	(present 1st and 3rd singular of *slæpan*)

Adverbs

eft   afterwards

næfre   never

þider   thither

Prepositions

on   on, into

Adjectives

sum   one

Ðā   then

Conjunction

and   and

Demonstrative Pronoun

sē   the

Chapter 7 Translation Practice

1. Slǣpþ hē nǣfre.

2. Sum mann fēoll on īse.

3. Ðā hīe ðider cōmon.

4. Sē kyng geaf gryþ Olāfe.

5. And hē āstah on heofonas.

6. Hē eft gebēte.

8

OVERVIEW OF VERBS

The simplest grammatical sentences require a **subject** (which can be a pronoun or a noun) and a **verb**. In the next chapter we will learn some irregular verbs. This chapter is designed to familiarize you with the various roles verbs can play in a sentence.

Verbs are action words, expressing things that happen.

Alfred <u>ruled</u> the West Saxon people.

"Ruled" is the verb in the sentence.

There are several kinds of verbs:

Main verbs: These verbs express the main action of a sentence or clause:

Alfred <u>ruled</u> the West Saxon people.

Auxiliary Verbs: These verbs (sometimes known as **helping verbs**) are combined with the main verb:

Alfred <u>had</u> <u>ruled</u> the West Saxon people for ten years.

"<u>Had</u>" is an auxiliary linked to the main verb, "<u>ruled</u>."

Linking Verbs : These verbs ("is," "was," "are" and other forms of the verb "to be") are used to rename or describe a subject; one useful way to analyze them is to think of linking verbs as being the same as an equals sign (=) between two things:

Alfred <u>is</u> a king.

"King" is called a **subject complement** or **predicate nominative**. It renames "Alfred" and is therefore separated from "Alfred" by the linking verb "was." A subject complement will be the same **case** (the **nominative**) as the noun it renames.

Modal Verbs : These verbs (also known as **modal auxiliaries**) can be used to indicate additional information about the verb:

Alfred <u>could</u> <u>defeat</u> the Vikings.

"Could" is a **modal** verb modifying "defeat." "Might," "must," "should" and "would" are some of the most common modal verbs (use "coulda, woulda, shoulda" as a mnemonic for modals).

Infinitives : These verbs indicate action that can happen at any point in time (hence, "infinitive").

In Modern English they are constructed by adding the word "to" to the root form of the verb.

Alfred learned that it is difficult <u>to rule</u> a fragmented nation.

Alfred learned something about ruling in general that could be applied to any person in any time.

Note: Verbs are listed in dictionaries and glossaries under their infinitive forms.

Participles are verbs used as adjectives:

Alfred's <u>aching</u> back caused him much pain.

"Aching" is a verb ("ache" + ing) used as an adjective (it modifies the noun "back"). This is an example of a **present participle** because the "-ing" form is in the **present tense**.

Alfred's <u>tired</u> eyes limited the reading he could do.

"Tired" is a verb ("tire" + d) used as an adjective (it modifies the noun "back"). Because it is in the **past tense**, it is a **past participle**.

Gerunds are verbs used as nouns.

<u>Reading</u> was Alfred's favorite leisure activity.

"Reading" is a verb ("read" + ing) used as a noun (it is the subject of the sentence).

Inflected Infinitives: Some grammar books call this the "Old English Gerund," which is not precisely correct but gives the idea of what the inflected infinitive is communicating. Regularly preceded by the Old English preposition *to*, the inflected infinitive is a verb form generally used to express the idea of *purpose*:

Alfred sent troops <u>to guard</u> the bridge.

The reason the troops were sent was to accomplish the purpose expressed by the infinitive "to guard." Another way of translating, one that preserves the gerundive "feel" of the word, would be "for guarding" or "for the purpose of guarding."

You can almost always translate the inflected infinitive as a Modern English infinitive. For example:

Infinitive : *bewerien* = to guard
Inflected infinitive : *tō bewerienne* = for the purpose of guarding

The specific forms of inflected infinitives are listed in the paradigm for each verb.

Conjugating

Like Modern English verbs, Anglo-Saxon verbs change form depending upon who performs an action (the **person** of the verb), how many perform the action (the **number** of the verb), whether the action was in the past or the present (the **tense** of the verb), and whether the verb is a statement, command, or prediction (the **mood** of the verb). Writing out the various forms of a verb for each of its possible grammatical uses is called **conjugating** the verb.

In Modern English, we recognize three **persons** and two **numbers** for a verb:

Person	Singular	Plural
1st	**I**	**we**
2nd	**you**	**you** (plural: "y'all" or "younz")
3rd	**he , she**, **it**	**they**

Although we recognize past, present and future tenses in Modern English, Old English does not have a future tense. (One bad joke Anglo-Saxonists sometimes make is: "Old English: there's no future in it.") Old English communicates the idea of future happenings with the present tense and the **subjunctive mood** (discussed below).

For the Modern English verb "to walk," we conjugate as follows:

Present Tense

Person	Singular	Plural
1st	I walk	we walk
2nd	you walk	you ("y'all") walk
3rd	she walks, he walks, it walks	they walk

Past Tense

Person	Singular	Plural
1st	I walked	we walked
2nd	you walked	you ("y'all") walked
3rd	she walked, he walked, it walked	they walked

Luckily, you don't have to memorize the entire **paradigm** in order to learn the verb. For Modern English we only need to know:

- The **stem** of the verb: The **stem** of a verb is the underlying root form of the word. For **weak verbs** it is unchanged regardless of the word's grammatical function. It is the part of the verb onto which **endings** are attached.

- The **ending** "s" for third person singular present tense.

- The **ending** "ed" to indicate all past tenses.

Thus our simplified **paradigm** for "to walk" would be:

To the stem "walk" add:

Present Tense

Person	Singular	Plural
1st	-	-
2nd	-	-
3rd	s	-

(the dash means that there is no **ending** added to the **stem**)

Past Tense

Person	Singular	Plural
1st	ed	ed
2nd	ed	ed
3rd	ed	ed

Mood

We also recognize three **moods** in verbs:

1. The **indicative** mood is used for statements: "I walk quickly."

2. The **imperative** mood is used for commands: "Walk to the store!"

3. The **subjunctive** mood is used for predictions or possibilities and can indicate hypothetical statements or obligations. In Modern English we often use a **modal** or an **if-clause** to indicate a subjunctive: "I <u>might</u> walk to the store later." "I <u>could</u> walk to the store tomorrow." "<u>If I were</u> to walk to the store, I would get that for you."

Verb Classes

Old English verbs can be divided into four main categories:

1. **Weak verbs** , in which endings are added to a **stem** to indicate different **persons, numbers,** and **tenses**: walk /walk<u>ed</u> is a Modern English example. Weak verbs are the subject of Chapter 16.

2. **Strong verbs,** in which a vowel in the verb stem is changed to indicate different tenses: r<u>i</u>ng / r<u>a</u>ng is a Modern English example. Strong verbs are the subject of Chapter 17.

3. **Preterite-Present verbs,** which combine features of both strong and weak verbs (strong past tenses are shifted to present and weak endings are used in the past tense). Preterite-Present Verbs are the subject of Chapter 18.

4. **Irregular verbs,** such as "to be" and "to go," which do not follow the major patterns. We will cover the most important irregular verbs in Chapter 9.

9

IRREGULAR VERBS

At the very minimum a grammatical sentence requires a subject and a verb. We can use the **personal pronouns** from Chapter 7 for subjects, and now we will add verbs to them to make our first sentences in Old English.

The first verbs we learn are **irregular verbs** (verbs which are **conjugated** differently from most verbs in the language). There are two reasons to begin with the irregular verbs: first, they're very common (verbs like "is", "do" and "go" are all irregular in Anglo-Saxon). Second, you can just memorize them as a group without having to worry (yet) about working through conjugation patterns.

The four most important Old English irregular verbs are:

> *bēon* = to be
> *willan* = to wish
> *dōn* = to do
> *gān* = to go

Bēon ("to be")

Bēon is a special case because it has <u>two forms</u> in the present tense (*eom* and *bēo*). These correspond (very roughly) with Modern English "is" and "be" (*eom* is the antecedent of Modern English "am" and *beo* is the antecedent of Modern English "be").

Although Old English does not have a future tense, a good rule of thumb is that the *eom* forms are generally **present tense** while *bēon* forms *may* indicate **future tense** (you'll need to use the context of the sentence to be sure of the implied tense).

Indicative Mood

	Present	Present	Past
1st Person Singular (I)	eom	bēo	wæs
2nd Person Singular (you)	eart	bist	wǣre
3rd Person Singular (he, she, it)	is	bið	wæs
Plurals (all three persons)	sind , sint, sindon	bēoð	wǣron

Subjunctive Mood

	Present	Present	Past
Singulars (all three persons)	sīe	bēo	wǣre
Plurals (all three persons	sīen	bēon	wǣren

Imperative Mood

	Present Only
Second Person Singular (you)	bēo or wes
Second Person Plural (y'all)	bēoð or wesað

> **Note**: The imperative occurs only in the present tense and in the second person.

Inflected infinitive: **tō bēonne**

Participles: **bēonde, wesende**

Willan ("to wish")

> Translating tip: One of the most common mistakes students make in beginning Old English is to translate forms of *willan* as "will" rather than "wish." This mistake is natural given the lack of a future tense in Old English, but you need to avoid it by remembering that willan, although it looks like "will," is a false friend and should not be relied upon. Memorize: *willan* means "to wish," not "will."

Indicative Mood

	Present	Past
1st Person Singular (I)	**wille , wile**	**wolde**
2nd Person Singular (you)	**wilt**	**woldest**
3rd Person Singular (he, she, it)	**wille** or **wile**	**wolde**
Plurals (all three persons)	**willað**	**woldon**

Subjunctive Mood

	Present	Past
All Singulars	**wille** or **wile**	**wolde**
All Plurals	**willen**	**wolden**

Imperative Mood

	Present Only
Second Person Plural only ("y'all")	**nyllað** or **nellað**

> **Note**: The imperative form of *willan* is only used with the negative prefix *ne* replacing *w* (this is a contracted form of *ne willan*). In Old English one can command a group of people not to wish for something, but not to wish for something.

Present participle: **willende** ("wishing")

Dōn ("to do")

Indicative Mood

	Present	Past
1st Person Singular (I)	dō	dyde
2nd Person Singular (you)	dēst	dydest
3rd Person Singular (he, she, it)	dēþ	dyde
Plurals (all three persons)	dōð	dydon

Subjunctive Mood

	Present	Past
All Singulars	dō	dyde
All Plurals	dōn	dyden

Imperative Mood

	Present only
Second Person Singular (you)	dō
Second Person Plural ("y'all")	dōð

Inflected infinitive: **tō dōnne**

Present participle: **dōnde**

Past participle: **dōn**

Gān ("to go")

Indicative Mood

	Present	Past
1st Person Singular (I)	gā	ēode
2nd Person Singular (you)	gǣst	ēodest
3rd Person Singular (he, she, it)	gǣð	ēode
Plurals (all three persons)	gāð	ēodon

Subjunctive Mood

	Present	Past
All Singulars	gā	ēode
All Plurals	gān	ēoden

Imperative Mood

	Present only
Second Person Singular (you)	gā
Second Person Plural ("y'all")	gāð

Inflected infinitive: **tō gānne**

Present participle: **gānde**

Past participle: **gān**

> **Some patterns to recognize**: Although the verbs given above are **irregular**, it is not too early to start noticing some patterns. For example, the second person singular has the ending -*st*, the third person singular has the ending -*ð*, and the plurals have the ending -*að*. Subjunctives are characterized by having -*e* in the ending (*en* and *e*).

Chapter 9 Vocabulary

Learn these words in addition to memorizing the irregular verbs.

Nouns

ceastre	city, walled town	(accusative case)
Cerdice	Cerdic	(proper name; dative case)
duru	door	(accusative case)
mǣgas	kinsmen	(nominative case; plural of *mǣg*)
ryhtfæderencyn	direct paternal ancestry	(nominative case)
seledrēamas	hall-joys	(nominative case, plural of *seledrēam*)
unwrītere	bad scribe	(nominative case)
wræcca	exile	(nominative case)
yfel	evil, harm	(accusative case)

Prepositions

on	in, into
mid	with
tō	to

Demonstrative Pronouns

sē	the	(masculine, singular, nominative)
þā	that, the	(feminine, singular, accusative)

Adverbs

hwǣr	where

hwī	why
swā	so
þā	then
ūt	out

Chapter 9 Translation Practice

1. Ðā ēodon hīe ūt.

2. Hwǣr sindon seledrēamas?

3. Hē on þā duru ēode.

4. Hiera mǣgas him mid wǣron.

5. Hē wrǣcca wæs.

6. Hīe þā swā dydon.

7. Yfel dēþ sē unwrītere.

8. Gā on þā ceastre.

9. Hiera ryhtfæderencyn gǣþ tō Cerdice.

10. Hwī dēst þū swā?

Chapter 9 Reading Practice

Try to read and understand the following paragraph without translating it word for word. See how much you can understand before you look at the translation below. Remember that Tyronian note (&) means "and." "xxx" is the Roman numeral 30.

From the *Anglo-Saxon Chronicle* entry for the year 900 :

Hēr gefōr ælfred Āþulfing syx nihtum ǣr ealra hāligra mæssan. Sē wæs cyning ofer eall Ongelcyn būtan þǣm dǣle þe under Dena onwalde wæs, & hē hēold þæt rīce ōþrum healfum lǣs þe xxx wintra. & þā fēng Ēadweard his sunu tō rīce.

Here departed [died] King Alfred, six nights before the mass of all saints [All Hallows Day, November 1]. He was king over all England except that part which was ruled under the Danes, and he held his kingdom one and a half [years] less than thirty winters. And then his son Edward took the throne.

10

DEMONSTRATIVE AND RELATIVE PRONOUNS

This is perhaps the most important chapter in this grammar book. **Demonstrative** and **relative pronouns** are two of the major sticking points for students of Old English. If you take some extra time with this chapter and make sure that you understand the concepts behind these two kinds of pronouns, and if you make sure that you memorize the paradigms and can recognize them, you will be well on your way to being able to translate Old English sentences fluently.

Demonstrative pronouns are "pointing words": they indicate relationships of proximity.

> Alfred gave <u>this</u> jewel to the bishop and <u>that</u> one to his ealdorman.

"This," "that," "these" and "those" are demonstrative pronouns (Mnemonic tip: "<u>D</u>emonstratives: <u>d</u>is, <u>d</u>at, <u>d</u>ese and <u>d</u>ose). They demonstrate (point out) nouns.

The words that translate as "a," "an" and "the" are also considered to be demonstratives in Anglo-Saxon (we call them **articles** in Modern English). Why? Because in Old English *sē* ("the") can stand by itself and doesn't need a noun to follow it; therefore it gains pronoun status.

For example: "Who did it?" / "The man did it" is perfectly acceptable in Modern English. In Old English, however, you can leave out "man": "Who did it?" / "*Sē* did it." This sentence could be translated as "*The* did it," but because *sē* indicates the masculine gender, we can translate it as "The masculine one did it" and therefore "He did it."

Sometimes in Old English a demonstrative will be followed by a noun, and you can then translate the demonstrative as "the" or "that" or "a." But other times you will need to supply a noun or **noun phrase** such as "the one" or "that one."

Remember that demonstrative pronouns are providing you with useful information about the **case** of a word, thus telling you if the demonstrative and the word it is describing (if it is describing a word) is a **subject**, **object** or **possessive**. Demonstrative pronouns are thus very helpful for determining the grammatical construction of a sentence.

Note: Demonstrative pronouns have <u>five</u> (rather than four) case forms. The **instrumental** case is here actually different from the **dative**.

Demonstrative Pronouns Paradigms

Singular Demonstrative Pronouns: The, That

Case	Masculine	Neuter	Feminine
Nominative	sē	þæt	sēo
Genitive	þæs	þæs	þære
Accusative	þone	þæt	ðā
Dative	þām or þǣm	þām or þǣm	þære
Instrumental	þȳ or þon	þȳ or þon	

Plural Demonstrative Pronouns: The, Those

Case	All Three Genders
Nominative	þā
Genitive	þāra or þǣra
Accusative	þā
Dative and Instrumental	þām or þǣm

Singular Demonstrative Pronouns: This

Case	Masculine	Neuter	Feminine
Nominative	þēs	þis	þēos
Genitive	þises or þisses	þises or þisses	þisse or þeosse
Accusative	þisne	þis	þās
Dative	þisum or þissum	þisum or þissum	þisse or þeosse
Instrumental	þȳs or þīs	þȳs or þīs	

Plural Demonstrative Pronouns: These

Case	All Three Genders
Nominative	þās
Genitive	þissa or þeossa
Accusative	þās
Dative and Instrumental	þisum , þissum, þeosum, þeossum

Relative Pronouns

The relative pronouns are the second key to translating Old English successfully. A significant portion of student frustration with translating comes from sentences that use relatives. If you take some extra time to understand these pronouns you will save yourself some later irritation.

First we need to introduce the grammatical concept of a **clause**. A clause is a **dependent** part of a sentence that has its own **subject** and **predicate** but still depends on the main part of the sentence (a predicate can be simply a verb, or it can include a verb and an object). A **relative clause** is a clause that modifies a noun or a pronoun elsewhere in the sentence.

For example, in the sentence

> Alfred was the leader <u>who defeated the Vikings</u>.

"who defeated the Vikings" is a relative clause that modifies (describes) "leader."

The clause "who defeated the Vikings" is called **relative** because it renames or explains a **noun** in the sentence: "who" is relative (in this case) to "leader."

In Anglo-Saxon there is a **relative particle**, *þe*, which (mercifully) has the same form for all cases, numbers and genders. The relative particle is often combined with one of the **demonstrative** or

personal pronouns to indicate the gender, number and case of the thing being described.

> Translation Tip : Students often get confused in translating because they translate *þe* as "the" (which is understandable, since they sound similar). If you make an effort to automatically translate *þe* as "which," you won't have this problem. Memorize: *þe* never means "the."

It is often easiest to approximately translate a relative pronoun as "which" to get the general idea of the grammatical structure of the sentence. Once you have that structure in mind you can figure out whether to refine your translation to "which," "that," "who" or "whom."

Often a demonstrative pronoun comes immediately before *þe* in the sentence, for example, *þone þe* or *sē þe*.

Sometimes the relative particle *þe* will be omitted and the demonstrative alone will have to be translated as a relative. For example, *þone*. These constructions are the ones that most frequently confuse students; you'll have to use the context of the sentence to determine if you have a garden-variety **demonstrative** (which is usually followed by an adjective or adjective-noun combination) or a **relative** (which may be followed by a complex clause). In all cases you are safe translating a relative as "which."

Some examples of the use of *þe* as a relative pronoun:

> This is the sword *þe* I found. (<u>which</u> I found)

> They were the people *þe* we went with. (<u>whom</u> we went with).

> We climbed the mountain *þe* was in Wales. (<u>which</u> was in Wales).

Adding demonstrative pronouns to *þe*:

This is the friend *þȳ þe* I will talk: (<u>with whom</u> I will talk).

Give it to him, *þone þe* I called. (<u>the one whom</u> I called).

Alfred ate the cakes, *þā þe* he was given. (<u>those which</u> he was given)

Demonstrative pronouns used as relatives without *þe*:

He is the scholar *þȳ* I will meet: (<u>with whom</u> I will meet).

Carry it to him, *þone* I pointed out. (<u>he whom</u> I pointed out).

Wulfgar blessed the wine and bread, *þā* he was given. (<u>those which</u> he was given)

For þām þe . One of the biggest translating headaches for beginning students of Anglo-Saxon is the idiom *for þām þe* and its various related forms such as *for þone þe*. It is no use trying to explain the reasons why this motley collection of a **preposition**, a **demonstrative** and a **relative particle** means "because." Simply memorize that *for þām þe* (and *for þām*) and similar forms should be translated as "because."

Chapter 10 Vocabulary

Nouns

andswere	answer	(direct object; feminine accusative singular)
aþās	oaths	(accusative plural)
cyning	king	(nominative)
ēaran	ears	(plural of *ēare*, neuter accusative)
Ēastengle	East Angles	(nominative plural; proper name)
ēastrīce	east kingdom	(dative)

gēare	year	(instrumental)
Godes	of God	(genitive singular)
gōdum	with goods	(dative plural)
herenesse	in praise	(dative singular)
Ifling	the River Ifling	(nominative)
lār	teaching, doctrine	(nominative)
mere	lake, body of water	(dative)
mōnað	months	(nominative plural)
mynster	monastery	(accusative)
Norþymbre	Northumbrians	(nominative plural; proper name)
Ōswold	Oswald	(nominative; proper name)
rōd	cross, rood	(nominative)
Scyppendes	of the Creator	(genitive singular)
staþe	shore, bank	(dative)
tīde	time	(accusative)
Trūso	Truso	(name of a city; nominative)
twelf	twelve	(nominative; number)
(ge)weorc	defensive work, fort	(accusative)
weoruldhāde	secular life	(dative)
word	word	(accusative)
wurþmynte	reverence, honor	(dative)
ylde	old age	(genitive)

Verbs

ārǣrde	erected	(past 3rd person singular of *ārǣran*)
bodad	preached	(past participle of *bodian*)

77

cwæþ	said	(past 3rd person singular of [*ge*]*cweþan*)
cymeþ	comes	(present 3rd person singular of *cuman*)
gehȳranne	hearing	(inflected infinitive of *gehīeran*)
gehȳraþ	hear	(present 3rd person plural of *gehīeran*)
gehȳre	hear	(singular imperative of *gehīeran*)
gesēoh	see	(imperative singular of *gesēon*)
geseted	set, placed, located	(past 3rd person singular of *gesettan*)
hæbbe	have	(present 3rd person subjunctive of *habban*)
hæfdon	had	(past 3rd person plural of *habban*)
herian	to praise	(infinitive)
onfēng	took, received	(past 3rd person singular of *onfōn*)
ongan	began	(past 3rd person singular of *onginnen*)
(*ge*)*seald*	gave	(past participle of [*ge*]*sellan*)
singan	to sing	(infinitive)
standeþ	stands	(present 3rd person singular of *standan*)
stōd	stood	(past 3rd person singular of *standan*)
þafode	agreed	(past 3rd person singular of *þafian*)
(*ge*)*worht*	wrought, made	(past participle of [*ge*]*wyrcan*)
yflode	harmed	(past 3rd person singular of *yfelian*)

Adjectives

ylce	same
hwelc	of what sort

gelȳfdre	advanced	(genitive, feminine)
(ge)sāwene	visible	(past participle functioning as adjective)
unscyldig	un-guilty, sinless, innocent	

Adverbs

nū	now
siþþan	afterwards
sōna	soon, immediately
þǣr	there
þonne	then
wel	well

Prepositions

ofer	over
oþ	until
tō	for
ymb	about, around, approximately

Chapter 10 Translation Practice

1. Sēo ylce rōd siþþan, þe Ōswold þǣr ārǣrde, on wurþmynte þǣr stōd.

2. Gesēoh þū, cyning, hwelc þēos lār sīe þe ūs nū bōdad is.

3. Wæs hē, sē mon, in weoruldhāde geseted oþ þā tīde þe hē wæs gelȳfdre ylde.

4. Ðonne cymeþ Ifling of þǣm mere þe Trūso standeþ in staþe.

5. Ic wolde helpan þæs þe þǣr unscyldig wǣre, ond ne hērian þone þe hine yflode.

6. And þā þe gesāwene synt ofer þæt gōde land, ðā synd ðe þæt word gehȳraþ.

7. And hē cwæþ, "Gehȳre, sē þe ēaran hæbbe tō gehȳranne."

8. Þā hē þā þās andswere onfēng, ðā ongan hē sōna singan, in herenesse Godes Scyppendes.

9. Hē þæt wel þafode, and hēo hine in þæt mynster onfēng mid his gōdum.

10. On þȳs gēare-þæt wæs ymb twelf mōnað þæs þe hīe on þǣm, ēastrīce geweorc geworht hæfdon-Norþhymbre ond Ēastengle hæfdon Ælfrede cyninge āþas geseald.

Chapter 10 Reading Practice

Hēr lǣdde Bēocca aldormon Wesseaxna ælmessan & ælfredes cyninges tō Rōme. & æþelswiþ cūen, sīo wæs ælfredes sweostor cyninges, forþfērde, & hire līc līþ æt Pāfian. & þȳ ilcan gēare æþelred ercebiscep & æþelwold aldormon forþfērdon on anum mōnþe.

On þissum gēare næs nan færeld tō Rōme, būton tuēgen hlēaperas ælfred cyning sende mid gewrītum.

From the *Anglo-Saxon Chronicle* entry for the year 888 :

> Beocca the Ealdorman took the donations of the West Saxons and of King Alfred to Rome. And Queen Athelswith, who was King Alfred's sister, went forth (i.e., died), and her body lies at Pavia. And this same year Archbishop Athelred and Ealdorman Athelwold passed away in one month.

From the *Anglo-Saxon Chronicle* entry for the year 889 :

> In this year there was no journey to Rome, except by two messengers whom King Alfred sent with writings (letters).

STRONG ADJECTIVES

Adjectives are words used to describe nouns.

> Alfred was a <u>great</u> king.

"great" describes the noun "king," so it is an adjective.

There are two classes of adjectives in Old English, **strong adjectives**, which are the subject of this chapter, and **weak adjectives**, which we cover in the next chapter. Almost all Old English adjectives can be either strong or weak, depending on how they are used in a sentence. That's right: the same word is a strong adjective in some contexts and a weak adjective in others. Fortunately the rules for determining whether an adjective is strong or weak are very simple, and in any event, **strong** and **weak** are just labels that tell you what ending the adjective takes depending on the **case** (which, you'll remember, marks the grammatical function) of the noun it is modifying.

> **Strong adjectives** can stand on their own; they do not need a **demonstrative** to assist them.

    <u>Wise</u> kings are kind to their subjects.

Notice there is no **demonstrative** assisting the adjective. "Wise" is therefore, in this sentence, a **strong** adjective.

If an adjective has a **demonstrative** assisting it, it will be **weak**. If the same adjective has no **demonstrative**, it will be **strong**. If the sentence read: "<u>The</u> wise king is kind to his subjects," "wise" would be a **weak** adjective.

This characteristic of Old English adjectives is important, because there are different **declensions** that are used depending on whether or not an adjective is used in a grammatically **strong** or **weak** manner.

> <u>**Reminder**</u>: A **declension** is simply a list of the different endings that are added to a **stem** to indicate that the word is in a certain **case** (i.e., that it is fulfilling a certain grammatical function). A **declension** is for nouns, pronouns and adjectives what a **conjugation** is for verbs.

Strong Declension Adjectives Paradigms

Singular Strong Declension Adjectives Paradigm

Case	Masculine	Neuter	Feminine
Nominative	-	-	**u** or -*
Genitive	**es**	**es**	**re**
Accusative	**ne**	-	**e**
Dative	**um**	**um**	**re**
Instrumental	**e**	**e**	**re**

(A dash indicates that the stem gets no ending.)

Plural Strong Declension Adjectives Paradigm

Case	Masculine	Neuter	Feminine
Nominative	e	u *	a
Genitive	ra	ra	ra
Accusative	e	u or -*	a
Dative and Instrumental	um	um	um

***Note**: for strong adjectives with a long vowel (such as *gōd*), the nominative singular feminine and the accusative plural neuter have no endings (strong adjectives with a short vowel have *u*). See the example *gōd* below.

Strong Declension Adjectives Examples

til = good (*til* has a short **stem vowel**)

Singular Strong Declension Adjectives: Examples

Case	Masculine	Neuter	Feminine
Nominative	til	til	tilu
Genitive	tiles	tiles	tilre
Accusative	tilne	til	tile
Dative	tilum	tilum	tilre
Instrumental	tile	tile	tilre

Plural Strong Declension Adjectives: Examples

Case	Masculine	Neuter	Feminine
Nominative	tile	tilu	tila
Genitive	tilra	tilra	tilra
Accusative	tile	tilu	tila
Dative and Instrumental	tilum	tilum	tilum

Note: The genitive personal pronouns (possessive pronouns) *min, þin, sin, eower, uncer* and *incer* (see Chapter 7) can be used as adjectives ("<u>My</u> sword is old," "Alfred spoke to <u>your</u> friend"). When **possessive pronouns** are used adjectivally, they are declined like the strong adjective *til* (good).

gōd = good (*gōd* has a long **stem** vowel)

Singular Strong Declension Adjectives: Examples

Case	Masculine	Neuter	Feminine
Nominative	**gōd**	**gōd**	**gōd**
Genitive	**gōdes**	**gōdes**	**gōdre**
Accusative	**gōdne**	**gōd**	**gōde**
Dative	**gōdum**	**gōdum**	**gōdre**
Instrumental	**gōde**	**gōde**	**gōdre**

Plural Strong Declension Adjectives: Examples

Case	Masculine	Neuter	Feminine
Nominative	**gōde**	**gōd**	**gōda, gōde**
Genitive	**gōdra**	**gōdra**	**gōdra**
Accusative	**gōde**	**gōd**	**gōda, gōde**
Dative and Instrumental	**gōdum**	**gōdum**	**gōdum**

Note: Adjectives in Old English *must* agree with the nouns they modify in terms of **case**, **gender** and **number** (i.e., if an adjective is in the genitive case, it can only be modifying a noun in the genitive case). You can use this principle of **case agreement** to help you match adjectives with their nouns. This is particularly useful when translating poetry.

Chapter 11 Reading Practice

& þȳ ilcan gēare ofer Ēastron. ymbe gang dagas oþþe ǣr, ætēowde sē steorra þe mon on bōclǣden hǣt comēta, Sume men cweþaþ on Englisc þæt hit sīe feaxede steorra. forþǣm þǣr stent lang leoma of, hwīlum on ane healfe hwīlum on ǣlce healfe.

From the *Anglo-Saxon Chronicle* entry for the year 891 :

And this same year after Easter, around "going days" [Rogationtide][1] or earlier, appeared the star which men in book-Latin call "comet." Likewise men say in English that it is the "haired-star," because there stand out long beams of light at times on one side and at times on the other side.

87

12

WEAK ADJECTIVES

As we noted, there are two types of adjectives in Old English: **strong adjectives**, which we covered in the previous chapter, and **weak adjectives**. Almost all Old English adjectives can be either strong or weak, depending on how they are used in a sentence. **Strong** and **weak** are just labels that tell you what ending the adjective takes depending on the **case** (which, you'll remember, marks the grammatical function) of the noun it is modifying.

> **Weak adjectives** do not stand on their own; they come paired with a demonstrative.

     That wise king ruled Wessex.

In the example sentence "wise" is a weak adjective; the demonstrative pronoun "that" is paired with it. "That wise king" forms a single compound subject with all three words in the nominative case.

Weak Declension Adjectives Paradigms

Singular Weak Declension Adjectives Paradigm

Case	Masculine	Neuter	Feminine
Nominative	a	e	e
Genitive	an	an	an
Accusative	an	e	an
Dative and Instrumental	an	an	an

Plural Weak Declension Adjectives Paradigm

Case	All Three Genders
Nominative	an
Genitive	ra, ena
Accusative	an
Dative and Instrumental	um

Weak Declension Adjectives Examples

gōd = good (*gōd* has a long **stem** vowel)

Singular Weak Declension Adjectives: Examples

Case	Masculine	Neuter	Feminine
Nominative	gōda	gōde	gōde
Genitive	gōdan	gōdan	gōdan
Accusative	gōdan	gōde	gōdan
Dative and Instrumental	gōdan	gōdan	gōdan

Note: The *an* ending is a fairly reliable indication of the weak declensions (in both adjectives and nouns).

Plural Weak Declension Adjectives: Examples

Case	All Three Genders
Nominative	**gōdan**
Genitive	**gōdra, gōdena**
Accusative	**gōdan**
Dative and Instrumental	**gōdum**

Chapter 12 Vocabulary

Nouns

bisceop	bishop	(nominative)
burhware	citizenry	(accusative of *burhwaru*)
Finnum	Finns	(dative of *Finnas*)
Hēahmund	Heahmund	(proper name; nominative)
hrānas	reindeer	(accusative plural of *hrān*)
hūs	house	(nominative)
hwæl	whale	(nominative)
hwalas	whales	(plural accusative)
land	land, country	(nominative)
lande	land, country	(dative)
mannum	men	(dative plural of *man[n]*)
monna	men	(genitive plural of *man[n]*)
mynstermen	monks	(nominative plural of *mynsterman[n]*)
nēaweste	vicinity, neighborhood	(dative)

Verbs

fōð	catch, capture	(present plural of *fōn*)
wearð	became	(past singular 1st and 3rd person of *weorðan*)
wurdon	became	(past plural of *weorðan*)

Adjectives

āfyrhte	frightened	(past participle acting as an adjective)
brādost	broadest	
bȳne	cultivated	
dȳre	dear, precious	
fela	many	
fyrst	first	
gōd	good	
gram	angry	
lǣssa	smaller	
lēoht	light, not heavy	
micel	great, much	
ofslægen	slain	(past participle acting as an adjective)
ōðre	other	
snel	quick	
spēdig	prosperous	
swift	swift	
untrum	unwell	
wilde	wild	

Adverbs

ēasteweard	in the east
micclum	greatly
micle	much
swȳð e	very
ðǣr	there

Conjunctions

ac	but
for ðǣm	because
ond	and
ðonne	than

Prepositions

in	in	
mid	with	(+ dative case)
wið	against	(sometimes "with")

Chapter 12 Translation Practice

1. And wearþ sē cyning swȳþe gram wiþ þā burhware.

2. Hē wæs swȳþe spēdig man.

3. Ac hē is snel and swift and swīþe lēoht.

4. Ðā wurdon þā mynstermen micclum āfyrhte.

5. Ond þǣr wearþ Hēahmund bisceop ofslægen ond fela gōdra monna.
   [*fela gōdra monna* is an example of a **partitive genitive** (discussed below in Chapter 19). In this case, translate as a simple plural.]

6. And þæt bӯne land is ēasteweard brādost.

7. Hē wæs mid þǣm fyrstum mannum on þǣm lande.

8. Sē hwæl biþ micle lǣssa þonne ōþre hwalas.

9. Ðā bēoþ swӯþe dӯre mid Finnum, for ðǣm hӯ fōþ þā wildan hrānas mid.

10. Wæs þǣr in nēaweste untrumra monna hūs.
    Hint: the subject is the last word in the sentence.

Chapter 12 Reading Practice

þā hīe þā fela wucena sǣton on twā healfe þǣre, & sē cyng wæs west on Defnum wiþ þone sciphere, þā wǣron hīe mid metelīeste gewǣgde, & hæfdon miclne dǣl þāra horsa freten. & þā ōþre wǣron hungre ācwolen. þā ēodon hīe ūt tō þǣm monnum þe on ēasthealfe þǣre wīcodon, & him wiþ gefuhton, & þā Crīstnan hæfdon sige.

From the *Anglo-Saxon Chronicle* entry for the year 893 :

When they had sat on both sides of that [of the river] for many weeks, and the king was in the west in Devon [fighting] against the pirate-army, they suffered lack of food and had eaten the greater portion of their horses, and the others were perishing with hunger. Then they went out to the men who were camped on the east side, and fought against them, and the Christians had the victory.

STRONG NOUNS

Noun Classes

Like adjectives and pronouns, Old English nouns are **declined**: different endings are attached to the **stem** of a word, and these endings indicate what **case** a word belongs to and therefore what grammatical function that word is fulfilling in a sentence.

Old English nouns are divided into three main groups, **strong, weak**, and **minor**, based on the noun's **stem** and the **endings** that each noun takes in different grammatical **cases**.

A useful rule of thumb is that nouns whose **stems** end with a **consonant** are **strong**, while nouns whose **stems** end with a **vowel** (except for *u*) are **weak**. We will learn the paradigms for weak nouns in the next chapter.

The strong declension is itself subdivided into first, second, and third **declensions**, which are also called "masculine," "neuter" and "feminine." Some grammar books give complicated and confusing explanations about how masculine nouns are often masculine words but sometimes not, and so forth in greater and more confusing complexity. Don't bother. If you just think of **masculine**, **neuter** and **feminine** as arbitrary names for categories (it would be better if they were called alpha, beta and gamma) then you won't get confused. We'll call the declensions **first declension**, **second declension** and **third declension** (weak nouns, which we will discuss in Chapter 14, are often called **fourth declension**); we'll also put in the masculine, neuter, and feminine labels since these are used frequently in dictionaries and editions of Old English texts.

First Declension (Masculine) Nouns

Although we will use **first declension** to label these nouns which end in **consonants**, other grammars, dictionaries and editions will call them **masculine**. You may think of this group of nouns as the "spear-stone-king" group, since all of those words have traditional "masculine" associations and all are masculine strong first declension nouns.

Some Strong First Declension (Masculine) Nouns:

Old English	Modern English
gār	spear
stān	stone
cyning	king
fugol	bird
drēam	joy

You'll find the endings for these nouns in the table below.

Strong First Declension (Masculine) Nouns Paradigm

Case	Singular	Plural
Nominative	-	**as**
Genitive	**es**	**a**
Accusative	-	**as**
Dative and Instrumental	**e**	**um**

(A dash indicates that the stem gets no additional ending.)

Strong First Declension (Masculine) Singulars: Examples

Case	Old English	Modern English
Nominative	**cyning**	king (subject)
Genitive	**cyninges**	of the king (possession)
Accusative	**cyning**	king (direct object)
Dative and Instrumental	**cyninge**	with the king (or indirect object)

Strong First Declension (Masculine) Plurals: Examples

Case	Old English	Modern English
Nominative	**cyningas**	kings (subject)
Genitive	**cyninga**	of the kings (possession)
Accusative	**cyningas**	kings (direct object)
Dative and Instrumental	**cyningum**	with the kings (or indirect object)

Strong Second Declension (Neuter) Nouns:

We'll use **second declension** to label these nouns which end in consonants but whose plurals use *u* instead of *as*. Other grammars and dictionaries will call these **neuter**.

Some Strong Second Declensions (Neuter) Nouns:

Old English	Modern English
scip	ship
riht	law
mægen	power
fæt	cup

The endings for these nouns are given in the table below.

Strong Second Declension (Neuter) Nouns Paradigm

Case	Singular	Plural
Nominative	-	**u**
Genitive	**es**	**a**
Accusative	-	**u**
Dative and Instrumental	**e**	**um**

(A dash in the paradigm indicates that the stem gets no additional ending.)

Note that the only real difference between the **first declension (masculine)** and **second declension (neuter)** ending occurs in the nominative and accusative plurals, which use *u*. The rest of the paradigm is the same for both first declension and second declension nouns.

98

Strong Second Declension (Neuter) Singulars: Examples

Case	Old English	Modern English
Nominative	**scip**	ship (subject)
Genitive	**scipes**	of the ship (possession)
Accusative	**scip**	ship (direct object)
Dative and Instrumental	**scipe**	with the ship (or indirect object)

Strong Second Declension (Neuter) Plurals: Examples

Case	Old English	Modern English
Nominative	**scipu**	ships (subject)
Genitive	**scipa**	of the ships (possession)
Accusative	**scipu**	ships (direct object)
Dative and Instrumental	**scipum**	with the ships (or indirect object)

Strong Third Declension (Feminine) Nouns

What we'll call **third declension** nouns, other grammars, dictionaries and editions may label as **feminine**. They include the Old English words for "help," "need" and "gift."

Some Strong Third Declension (Feminine) Nouns

Old English	Modern English
liornung	learning
þearf	need
rest	rest
gēoc	help
giefu	gift

You'll find the endings for these nouns in the following table.

Strong Third Declension (Feminine) Nouns Paradigm

Case	Singular	Plural
Nominative	-	**a** or **e**
Genitive	**e**	**a** or **ena**
Accusative	**e**	**a** or **e**
Dative and Instrumental	**e**	**um**

(A dash in the paradigm indicates that the stem gets no additional ending.)

Yes, there really are two possibilities for the nominative, genitive and accusative plurals.

Strong Third Declension (Feminine) Singulars: Examples

Case	Old English	Modern English
Nominative	**giefu**	gift (subject)
Genitive	**giefe**	of the gift
Accusative	**giefe**	gift (direct object)
Dative and Instrumental	**giefe**	with the gift (or indirect object)

Strong Third Declension (Feminine) Plurals: Examples

Case	Old English	Modern English
Nominative	**giefa**	gifts (subject)
Genitive	**giefena**	of the gifts
Accusative	**giefa**	gifts (direct object)
Dative and Instrumental	**giefum**	with the gifts (or indirect object)

The *ge* prefix

Some Old English nouns regularly appear with the prefix *ge* attached to them. This usually occurs in the plural and indicates some sort of jointness or togetherness about the noun, for example, *gebrōþru* ("brothers"). The *ge* prefix presents no difficulty to understanding a word, but it can cause problems when you are looking up words in a glossary or dictionary. If you have trouble finding a *ge* word, mentally delete the *ge* and look for the **stem** of the noun. Only search for the *ge* form if you are unable to find the correct stem.

Chapter 13 Vocabulary

Nouns

blōdgyte	bloodshed	(strong, masculine)
bryne	fire, burning	(strong, masculine)
(ge)bytlu	buildings	(strong, neuter; nominative plural)
(ge)dreccednes	tribulation	(strong, feminine)
earfoðnes	hardship	(strong, feminine)
gafol	profit, tribute, taxes	(strong, neuter)
gār	spear	(strong, masculine)
here	war, battle	(strong, masculine)
ieldran	ancestors	(strong, feminine; nominative plural)
mæden	maiden, girl	(strong, neuter)
stōw	place	(strong, feminine)
tēolung	area being farmed	(strong, feminine)

þegn	lord, nobleman	(strong, masculine)
werod	troop, company	(strong, neuter)
wīsdōm	wisdom	(strong, masculine)
woruld	world	(strong, feminine); often spelled *weoruld*

Verbs

becumað	happen, befall	(present 3rd person plural of *becuman*)
berȳpð	plunder	(present 3rd person singular of *berȳpan*)
dohte	availed	(past tense 3rd person singular of *dugan*)
gȳmð	cares for	(present 3rd person singular of *gīeman*; + genitive case)
hæfde	had	(past tense 3rd person singular of *habban*)
hīoldon	held	(past tense 3rd person plural of *healdan*)
lofodon	loved	(past tense 3rd person plural of *lufian*)
wagode	waved, shook	(past tense 3rd person singular of *wagian*)

Adverbs

ǣr	previously
grǣdelīce	greedily
lange	long, for long

Adjectives

micle	large
wanspēdig	poor, destitute

Conjunctions

ēac   also

ne...ne   neither...nor

New Forms of Pronouns

hīo   she

ðissere   this   (dative feminine singular)

Chapter 13 Translation Practice

1. Ne dohte hit nū lange ac wæs here and hunger, bryne and blōdgyte.

2. Hīo hæfde þǣr swīþe micle werod hire þegna and ēac ōþerra mǣdena.

3. Hē gȳmþ grǣdlīce his tēolunge, his gafoles, his gebytla; hē berȳpþ ðā wanspēdigan.

4. Fela gedreccednyssa and earfoþnyssa becumaþ on þissere worulde.

5. Ūre ieldran, ðā ðe ðās stōwe ǣr hīoldon, hīe lofodon wīsdōm.

Chapter 13 Reading Practice

þæs ymb .iiii. niht Æþelred Cyning & ælfred his brōþur þǣr micle fierd tō Readingum gelǣddon & wiþ þone here gefuhton. & þǣr wæs micle wæl geslægen on gehwæþre hond, & Æþelwulf Aldormon wearþ ofslægen, & þā Deniscan āhton wælstōwe gewald. & þæs ymb .iiii. niht gefeaht Æþelred Cyning & Ælfred his brōþur wiþ alne þone here on Æscesdūne, & hīe wǣrun on twǣm gefylcum: on ōþrum wæs Bachsecg & Halfdene þā hæþnan cyningas, & on ōþrum wǣron þā eorlas. & þā gefeaht sē cyning æþelred wiþ þāra cyninga getruman, & þǣr wearþ sē cyning Bagsecg ofslægen.

From the *Anglo-Saxon Chronicle* entry for the year 871:

Then four nights afterward king Athelred and Alfred his brother led a great army there into Reading and fought against the army [of the Danes]. And there was great slaughter on either hand, and Athelwulf the Ealdorman was slain, and the Danes had control over the place of slaughter. And after four nights King Athelred and Alfred his brother fought against the entire army at Ashdown, and they were in two groups: in the one was Bagsecg and Halfdane, the heathen kings, and in the other were the [Danish] earls. And then King Athelred fought against the troop of the kings, and there was King Bagsecg slain.

14

WEAK NOUNS

Fourth declension ("weak") nouns are nouns whose stems end in a vowel (except for nouns that end in *u*, which are either **third declension** or **minor declension**). You don't need to be concerned about the gender of fourth-declension nouns. Quite a number of fourth declension nouns are parts of the body.

Some Fourth Declension (Weak) Nouns

Old English	Modern English
blōstma	flower
draca	dragon
ēage	eye
sceaþa	enemy
hǣte	heat

The endings for these nouns are given in the table below.

Fourth Declension (Weak) Nouns Paradigm

Case	Singular	Plural
Nominative	-	an
Genitive	an	ena
Accusative	an	an
Dative and Instrumental	an	um

(A dash in the paradigm indicates that the stem gets no additional ending.)

Note that *an* covers all cases except the **genitive** and the **dative/instrumental** plural (with its ending of *um*).

Fourth Declension Weak Singulars: Examples

Case	Old English	Translation
Nominative	**draca**	dragon (subject)
Genitive	**dracan**	of the dragon
Accusative	**dracan**	dragon (direct object)
Dative and Instrumental	**dracan**	with the dragon (or indirect object)

Fourth Declension Weak Plurals: Examples

Case	Old English	Translation
Nominative	**dracan**	dragons (subject)
Genitive	**dracena**	of the dragons
Accusative	**dracan**	dragons (direct object)
Dative and Instrumental	**dracum**	with the dragons (or indirect object)

Chapter 14 Vocabulary

Nouns

beorhtnys	brightness	(strong, feminine)
carcerne	prison, jail	(strong, neuter, nom. pl. *carcern*)
cilde	child	(strong, neuter, nom. pl. *cild*)
earn	eagle	(strong, masculine)
hræfn	raven	(strong, masculine)
hrāw	corpse, flesh	(strong, neuter)
land, lond	land, country	(strong, neuter)
lāðgenīðla	foe, enemy	(weak, masculine)
lēoht	light	(strong, neuter)
mōna	moon	(weak, masculine)
sunne	sun	(weak, feminine)
tungol	star	(strong, neuter)
wōp	weeping	(strong, masculine)
wracu	suffering, pain	(strong, feminine, 3rd declension)

Verbs

befrīnað	ask	(imperative plural of *befrīnan*)
betȳndon	imprisoned	(past tense 3rd person plural of *betȳnan*)
(ge)biddan	pray to, ask	(infinitive)
bryttigean	to share	(infinitive)
cȳðað	make known	(imperative plural of *cȳÐan*)
faraþ	go	(imperative plural of *faran*)
lēton	left	(past tense 3rd person plural of *lǣtan*)
mæge	be able, may	(subjunctive 1st person singular of magan; preterite-present)
(ge)mētað	find	(present tense 2nd person plural of [ge]mētan)

| *styredon* | stirred, moved | (past tense 3rd person plural of *styrian*) |
| *(ge)worden* | become | (past participle of *weorÐan*) |

Adverbs

ardlīce	quickly
eft	afterwards
ne	not

Adjectives

eal	all
hasupād	grey-coated
hēan	poor
hyrnednebb	horn-beaked
gemǣne	common to
rīce	rich
salowigpād	dark-feathered
sweart	gloomy, dark, black

Prepositions

be	about, alongside
behindan	behind
on	in

Chapter 14 Translation Practice

1. Ðǣre sunnan beorhtnys, mōnan lēoht, and ealra tungla sind gemǣne þām rīcan and þām hēanan.

2. Ne is þǣr on þām londe lāþgenīþla, ne wōp ne wracu.

3. Lētan him behindan hrāw bryttigean salowigpādan, ðone
    sweartan hræfn, hyrnednebban, and ðone hasupādan earn.

4. Faraþ ardlīce, and befrīnað be ðām cilde, and þonne gē hit
    gemētað, cȳðað mē, þæt ic mæge mē tō him gebiddan.

5. Ðā geworden wæs þæt hīe hine eft betȳndon on þām
    carcerne.

Chapter 14 Reading Practice

Hēr cuōm sē here intō Escanceastre from Wērhām, & sē sciphere
sigelede west ymbūtan, & þā mētte hīe micel ȳst on sæ, & þǣr
forwearþ .cxx. scipa æt Swanawīc. & sē Cyning Ælfred æfter þām
gehorsudan here mid fierde rād oþ Exanceaster & hīe hindan
ofrīdan ne meahte ǣr hīe on þām fæstene wǣron þǣr him mon tō
ne meahte. & hīe him þǣr foregīslas saldon. swā fela swā hē habban
wolde, & micle āþas swōron, & þā gōdne friþ hēoldon.

From the *Anglo-Saxon Chronicle* entry for the year 877:

Here the [Danish] army came into Exeter from Wareham, and the
ship army [the pirates] sailed around west, and then they met a
great storm on the sea and there off Swanage one hundred and
twenty ships were destroyed. And King Alfred rode after the
horsemen with his armies to Exeter and they could not catch them
before they were inside the fortress where men might not get to
them. And they there gave him [Alfred] hostages there, as many as
he wished to have, and swore great oaths and then held a good
peace.

15

MINOR DECLENSION NOUNS

Minor declensions are so called because there are many fewer words that follow these patterns than follow the **strong** and **weak** declensions (declensions 1 through 4). Nevertheless, several important and common words follow these minor declensions and you need to be able to recognize them.

There are three important minor declensions: the *u*-**declension**, the *r*-**declension** ("family words") and the **radical consonant declension**.

u -Declension nouns

Most *u*-declension nouns end in *u*, although the *u*-declension does contain some other nouns that end in consonants but nevertheless follow the same paradigm as those that end in *u*. Remember that not all nouns that end in *u* fall into the *u*-declension as most are **3rd-declension** nouns such as *giefu*.

Some *u*- declension Nouns:

Old English	Modern English
sunu (masculine)	son
hond (feminine)	hand
wudu (masculine)	wood
weald (masculine)	forest
medu (masculine)	mead
fela (neuter)	much

The endings for these nouns are given in the following table.

u- declension Nouns Paradigm

Case	Singular	Plural
Nominative	- or **a**	**a** or **u**
Genitive	**a**	**a**
Accusative	- or **a**	**a** or **u**
Dative and Instrumental	**a** or **u**	**um**

(A dash in the paradigm indicates that the stem gets no additional ending.)

u-Declension Nouns, Singular Forms: Examples

Case	Old English	Translation
Nominative	**sunu**	son (subject)
Genitive	**suna**	of the son
Accusative	**sunu**	son (direct object)
Dative and Instrumental	**suna**	with the son (or indirect object)

u-Declension Nouns, Plural Forms: Examples

Case	Old English	Translation
Nominative	**sunu**	sons (subject)
Genitive	**suna**	of the sons
Accusative	**sunu**	sons (direct object)
Dative and Instrumental	**sunum**	with the sons (or indirect object)

r- Declension Nouns

These nouns include the "family words" such as "mother" and "father."

Some *r*- Declension Nouns:

Old English	Modern English
fæder	father
brōðor	brother
mōdor	mother
sweostor	sister

The endings for these nouns are given in the following table.

r- Declension Nouns Paradigm

Case	Singular	Plural
Nominative	-	**ru** or **ra** or **ras**
Genitive	- or **res**	**ra**
Accusative	-	**ru** or **ra** or **ras**
Dative and Instrumental	- or **er**	**um** or **rum**

(A dash in the paradigm indicates that the stem gets no additional ending.)

r- Declension Nouns, Singular Forms: Examples

Case	Old English	Translation
Nominative	**fæder**	father (subject)
Genitive	**fæderes**	of the father
Accusative	**fæder**	father (direct object)
Dative and Instrumental	**fæder**	with the father (or indirect object)

r-Declension Nouns, Plural Forms: Examples

Case	Old English	Translation
Nominative	**fæderas**	fathers (subject)
Genitive	**fædera**	of the fathers
Accusative	**fæderas**	fathers (direct object)
Dative and Instrumental	**fæderum**	with the fathers (or indirect object)

Note: these endings for the plural (*as, a, as, um*) are the same as those for the 1st declension masculine nouns.

Radical Consonant Declension Nouns

Radical Consonant Declension nouns are nouns whose vowels change in the noun stem (the way that Modern English "foot" changes to "feet" in the plural) either in addition to, or in place of, adding an ending to the stem.

Some Radical Consonant Declension Nouns:

Old English	Modern English
monn	man
fōt	foot
tōð	tooth
bōc	book

The endings for these nouns are given in the following table:

Radical Consonant Declension Nouns Paradigm

Case	Singular	Plural
Nominative	-	-
Genitive	es	a
Accusative	-	-
Dative and Instrumental	vowel changes from *o* to *e* monn / menn	um

(A dash in the paradigm indicates that the stem gets no additional ending.)

Radical Consonant Declension Nouns, Singular Forms: Examples

Case	Old English	Translation
Nominative	fōt	foot (subject)
Genitive	fōtes	of the foot
Accusative	fōt	foot (direct object)
Dative and Instrumental	fēt	with the foot (or indirect object)

Radical Consonant Declension Nouns, Plural Forms: Examples

Case	Old English	Translation
Nominative	fōt	feet (subject)
Genitive	fōta	of the feet
Accusative	fōt	feet (direct object)
Dative and Instrumental	fōtum	with the feet (indirect object)

Chapter 15 Vocabulary

Nouns

abbudyss	abbess	(strong, feminine)
byrne	byrnie, coat of mail	(weak, feminine)
gār	spear	(strong, masculine)
guma	man, hero	(weak, masculine)
gūðsearo	war-gear	(strong, neuter)
gyfe	gift	(strong, feminine)
mann, monn	man	(minor, masculine)
mōrfæsten	fastness in the moors	(strong, neuter)
sǣmann	seaman, seafarer	(minor, masculine)
searo	war-gear	(strong, neuter)
sumor	summer	(minor, masculine)
sūðrima	south-coast	(weak, masculine)
swēg	sound, music	(strong, masculine)
werod	troop	(strong, neuter)
wudu	wood, forest	(minor, masculine)

Verbs

clyppan	embrace, love	(infinitive)
fōr	went, fared	(past tense 3rd person singular of *faran*)
forwearð	perished	(past tense 3rd person singular of *forweorðan*)
hearpian	to harp	(infinitive)
hringdon	rang	(past tense 3rd person plural of *hringan*)
lufian	love, praise	(infinitive)

meahte	was able	(past tense 3rd person singular of *magan*)
stōdon	stood	(past tense 3rd person plural of *standan*)
styredon	stirred, moved	(past tense 3rd person plural of *styrian*)
wagode	waved, shook	(past tense 3rd person singular of *wagian*)

Adverbs

| *ætgædere* | together |
| *unīeþelīce* | with difficulty, uneasily |

Adjectives

eal all

ilca same (masculine; feminine and neuter form is *ilce*)

lȳtle little, small

Prepositions

be by, on, along

Conjunctions

ðæt so that

New Forms of Pronouns

hī themselves

Chapter 15 Translation Practice

1. Ðȳ ilcan sumera forwearþ nō læs þonne xx scipa mid monnum mid ealle be þām sūþriman.

2. Hē meahte hearpian þæt sē wudu wagode, ond ðā stānas hīe styredon for þȳ swēge.

3. Byrnan hringdon, gūþsearo gumena; gāras stōdon; sǣmanna searo, samod ætgædere.

4. Þā ongan sēo abbudysse clyppan and lufian þā Godes gyfe in þǣm menn.

5. Ond hē lȳtle werede unīeþelīce æfter wudum fōr ond on mōrfæstenum.

Chapter 15 Reading Practice

Hēr lǣdde Beornhelm abbud Westseaxna ælmessan tō Rōme & Ælfredes Cyninges. & Godrum, sē norþerna cyning forþferde, þæs fulluhtnama wæs æþelstān (sē wæs ælfredes cyninges godsunu). & hē būde on Ēastenglum, & þæt lond ǣrest gesæt. & þȳ ilcan gēare for sē here of Sigene tō Sant Laudan, þæt is butueoh Brettum & Francum, & Brettas him wiþ gefuhton, & hæfdon sige, & hīe bedrifon ūt on ane ēa, & monige ādrencton.

From the *Anglo-Saxon Chronicle* entry for the year 890 :

Here abbot Beornhelm took the donations of the West Saxons and of King Alfred to Rome. And Guthrum passed away, the northern king whose baptized name was Athelstan (he was King Alfred's godson). And he lived in East Anglia and [of the Danes] settled that land first. And in this same year the [Danish] army went from the Seine to St Lô, that is between the Bretons and the Franks, and the Bretons fought against them, and had victory, and drove them out into a river, and many were drowned.

16

WEAK VERBS

To prepare to learn the majority of Old English verbs, it is important to review the material we covered in Chapter 8, where we went over the different types of verbs and the grammatical roles they play. We strongly recommend that you go back and re-read that chapter now.

Remember that Old English verbs can be divided into four main categories: **weak verbs** (the subject of this chapter), **strong verbs** (the subject of chapter 17), **preterite-present verbs** (the subject of chapter 18), and **irregular verbs** (which we discussed in chapter 9).

Weak verbs are verbs which add an **ending** to a verb **stem** to indicate **person**, **number**, **tense** and **mood**.

Walk / Walked is an example of a weak verb.

Most verbs in Modern English behave like weak verbs.

To find the **stem** of an Old English verb, take the **infinitive** and subtract the ending *-an*. For example, the stem of the verb *dēman* = "to judge" is *dēm*.

- **First conjugation:** The **stem** ends in a **consonant** (these are the most common weak verbs).

- **Second conjugation:** The **stem** generally ends in a **vowel** (these are less common).

- **Third conjugation:** These verbs don't fit into the first two conjugations. Luckily there are only three that you need to worry about.

Reminder: verbs are listed in dictionaries and glossaries under their infinitive forms.

Subtract *-an* to find the **stem** of the verb.

Add the appropriate ending from the table below to the stem to form the conjugated verb.

First Conjugation Weak Verbs: Paradigms

First Conjugation Weak Verbs, Indicative Mood:

Present Tense

Singular	
1st Person (I)	e
2nd Person (you)	est
3rd Person (he, she, it)	eð
Plural	
1st, 2nd and 3rd Persons	að

Past Tense

Singular	
1st Person (I)	de
2nd Person (you)	dest
3rd Person (he, she, it)	de
Plural	
1st, 2nd and 3rd Persons	don

Note: The past tense singular endings are constructed by simply adding -*d* to the present tense singular endings.

First Conjugation Weak Verbs, Subjunctive Mood:

Present Tense

Singular	
1st, 2nd and 3rd Persons	e
Plural	
1st, 2nd and 3rd Persons	en

The key to recognizing subjunctives is to look for *e* where you would otherwise expect *a* or *o*.

Past Tense

Singular	
1st, 2nd and 3rd Persons	de
Plural	
1st, 2nd and 3rd Persons	den

Note: The only difference between the present and past tense subjunctive is the addition of *d* to the ending.

First Conjugation Weak Verbs, Imperative Mood:

Singular	
2nd Person	**stem minus final letter**
Plural	
2nd Person	**aþ**

Note: The **imperative mood** can only be in the 2nd person and only in present tense.

Inflected infinitive: **tō stem + anne**
Present participle: **stem + ende**
Past participle: **stem + ed**

Weak 1st Conjugation Verbs Examples

Infinitive: *dēman* = "to judge"

First Conjugation Weak Verbs, Indicative Mood: Examples

Present Tense

Singular	
1st Person (I)	**dēme**
2nd Person (you)	**dēmest**
3rd Person (he, she, it)	**dēmeð**
Plural	
1st, 2nd and 3rd Persons	**dēmað**

Past Tense

Singular	
1st Person (I)	dēmde
2nd Person (you)	dēmdest
3rd Person (he, she, it)	dēmde
Plural	
1st, 2nd and 3rd Persons	dēmdon

First Conjugation Weak Verbs, Subjunctive Mood: Examples

Present Tense

Singular	
1st, 2nd and 3rd Persons	dēme
Plural	
1st, 2nd and 3rd Persons	dēmen

Past Tense

Singular	
1st, 2nd and 3rd Persons	dēmde
Plural	
1st, 2nd and 3rd Persons	dēmden

First Conjugation Weak Verbs, Imperative Mood: Examples

Singular	
2nd Person	**dēm**
Plural	
2nd Person	**dēmaþ**

Inflected infinitive: **tō dēmanne**
Present participle: **dēmende**
Past participle: **dēmed**

Second Conjugation Weak Verbs

Second Conjugation verbs have -*ian* in the infinitive rather than -*an*.

As with all conjugations, you begin with the infinitive, which for second conjugation verbs ends in -*ian*. The infinitive is the form of the verb listed in the dictionary.

Subtract *ian* to find the **stem** of the verb. Add the endings in the table below to the stem to form the appropriate form of the verb.

Weak 2nd Conjugation Verbs Paradigms

Second Conjugation Weak Verbs, Indicative Mood:

Present Tense

Singular	
1st Person (I)	e
2nd Person (you)	ast
3rd Person (he, she, it)	að
Plural	
1st, 2nd and 3rd Persons	að

The major difference from the **first conjugation** is that *e* has been replaced with *a* in the 2nd and 3rd persons.

Past Tense

Singular	
1st Person (I)	ode
2nd Person (you)	odest
3rd Person (he, she, it)	ode
Plural	
1st, 2nd and 3rd Persons	odon

The only difference from the **first conjugation** is that *o* is added before the ending. For a few verbs *a* is added instead of *o*.

Second Conjugation Weak Verbs, Subjunctive Mood:

Present Tense

Singular	
1st, 2nd and 3rd Persons	ie
Plural	
1st, 2nd and 3rd Persons	ien

The only difference from the **first conjugation** is that *i* is added before the ending.

Past Tense

Singular	
1st, 2nd and 3rd Persons	ode
Plural	
1st, 2nd and 3rd Persons	oden

The only difference from the **first conjugation** is that *o* that is added before the ending.

Second Conjugation Weak Verbs, Imperative Mood:

Singular	
2nd Person	a
Plural	
2nd Person	iaþ

> **Note**: the **imperative mood** can only be in the 2nd person and only in present tense.

Inflected infinitive: **tō stem** + **ianne** (note: a few verbs use **eanne**)
Present participle: **iende** (note: a few verbs use **ende**)
Past participle: **od** (note: a few verbs use **d**)

Weak 2nd Conjugation Verbs Examples

The infinitive is "**bodian**" = "to proclaim." The stem is therefore "**bod**".

Second Conjugation Weak Verbs, Indicative Mood: Examples

Present Tense

Singular	
1st Person (I)	**bodie**
2nd Person (you)	**bodast**
3rd Person (he, she, it)	**bodað**
Plural	
1st, 2nd and 3rd Persons	**bodiað**

You'll notice that the only major difference from the first conjugation paradigm is that *e* has been replaced with *a* in the second and third persons.

Past Tense

Singular	
1st Person (I)	**bodode**
2nd Person (you)	**bododest**
3rd Person (he, she, it)	**bodode**
Plural	
1st, 2nd and 3rd Persons	**bododon**

The only difference from the **first conjugation** is that *o* is added before the ending. For a few verbs *a* is added instead of *o*.

Second Conjugation Weak Verbs, Subjunctive Mood: Examples

Present Tense

Singular	
1st, 2nd and 3rd Persons	bodie
Plural	
1st, 2nd and 3rd Persons	bodien

The only difference from the **first conjugation** is that *i* that is added before the ending.

Past Tense

Singular	
1st, 2nd and 3rd Persons	bodode
Plural	
1st, 2nd and 3rd Persons	bododen

The only difference from the **first conjugation** is that *o* that is added before the ending.

Second Conjugation Weak Verbs, Imperative Mood: Examples

Singular	
2nd Person	boda
Plural	
2nd Person	bodiað

Inflected infinitive: **to bodianne**
Present participle: **bodiende**
Past participle: **bodod**

Third Conjugation Weak Verbs

There are very few third conjugation weak verbs and they all have various quirks in their conjugations. Therefore instead of presenting a set of endings, this section will simply show the full conjugations for the three most common and important third conjugation verbs.

Infinitives:

habban = to have
libban (or *lifian*) = to live
secgan (or *secgean*) = to say

Weak 3rd Conjugation Verbs Paradigms

Weak 3rd Conjugation Verbs: Indicative Mood

Present Tense

Singular			
1st Person	hæbbe	libbe or lifge	secge
2nd Person	hafast or hæfast	lifast	sægst or segst
3rd Person	hafaþ or hæfþ	lifaþ	sægeþ or segþ
Plural			
1st, 2nd and 3rd Persons	habbaþ	libbaþ	secgaþ

Past Tense

Singular			
1st Person	hæfde	lifde	sægde or sæde
2nd Person	hæfdest	lifdest	sægdest or sædest
3rd Person	hæfde	lifde	sægde or sæde
Plural			
1st, 2nd and 3rd Persons	hæfdon	lifdon	sægdon or sædon

Weak 3rd Conjugation Verbs: Subjunctive Mood

Present Tense

Singular			
1st, 2nd and 3rd Persons	hæbbe	libbe	secge
Plural			
1st, 2nd and 3rd Persons	hæbben	libben	secgen

Past Tense

Singular			
1st, 2nd and 3rd Persons	hæfde	lifde	sægde or sæde
Plural			
1st, 2nd and 3rd Persons	hæfden	lifden	sægden or sæden

Weak 3rd Conjugation Verbs: Imperative Mood

Singular			
2nd Person	hafa	liofa	sage or sege
Plural			
2nd Person	habbað	libbað	secgað or secgeað

> **Note**: The **imperative mood** can only be in the second person and the present tense.

Weak 3rd Conjugation Verbs: Infinitives and Participles

Inflected Infinitives	tō habbanne	tō libbanne or tō lifienne	tō secganne or tō secgeanne
Present Participles	hæbbende	libbende or lifigende	secgende
Past Participles	hæfd	lifd	sægd or sǽd

Chapter 16 Vocabulary

Nouns

Ælfrede	Alfred	(proper name)
Andree	Andrew	(proper name)
apostoles	apostol	
āre	honor	
āþas	oaths	
biscop	bishop	
cyning	king	
cyricean	church	
Ēastengle	East Anglians	(proper name)
Finnas	Finns or Saami	(proper name)
gēare	year	
Godes	God	
lēasunga	false witness	
men	men	
mōrum	moors	
Norþhymbre	Northumbrians	
Paulīnus	Paulinus	(proper name)
reliquium	relic	(from the Latin infinitive *relinquere,* to leave behind)

Scæ	Saint	(abbreviation, taken from the Latin *sanctus*, saintly)
ðincg	thing	
þegenas	thanes	
Westsæ	West Sea	
word	word	

Verbs

bodade	proclaimed	(weak, 1st conjugation)
būde	dwelled	(irregular verb; infinitive *būan*)
cwæð	said	(weak, 3rd conjuagtion)
dēmen	would judge	(weak, 1st conjugation)
eardiaþ	dwell	(weak, 2nd conjugation)
(ge)earniaþ	deserve	(weak, 2nd conjugation)
efston	hastened	(weak, 1st conjugation)
elde	hesitated	(weak, 1st conjugation)
hæfdon	had	(weak, 3rd conjugation)
hæfst	have	(weak, 3rd conjugation)
(ge)hālgad	kept holy	(weak, 2nd conjugation)
lǣrde	taught	(weak, 1st conjugation)
(ge)lȳfanne	believe	(weak, first conjugation)
nele	does not wish	(negative of *willan*)
onscuna	avoid	(weak, 2nd conjugation)
recce	am interested in	(weak, 1st conjugation)
(ge)seald	given	(weak, 1st conjugation)
syle	give	(weak, 1st conjugation)
(ge)timbrade	would build	(weak, 1st conjugation)
wendon	went	(weak, 1st conjugation)
(ge)yrsian	to be angry	(weak, 2nd conjugation)

Adverbs

ā	always
forþ	forth
georne	eagerly
micclum	much
nū	now
swā	as
þā	then
þā gȳt	still (adverbial phrase)

Adjectives

ǣnig	any
hālgan	holy
norþweard	northward
unearge	brave
wlance	proud

Conjunctions

and	and
gif	if
ond	and

Prepositions

of	from
on	on

Chapter 16 Translation Practice

1. On þǣm mōrum eardiaþ Finnas.

2. Đā wendon forþ wlance þegenas; unearge men efston georne.

3. Onscuna þū ā lēasunga.

4. On þӯs gēare, Norþhymbre ond Ēastengle hæfdon Ælfrede cyninge āþas geseald.

5. Ne recce ic hwæt hī dēmen.

6. Paulīnus sē biscop Godes word bodade ond lǽrde ond sē cyning elde þā gӯt tō gelӯfanne.

7. Nū gif þū ǽnig ðincg hæfst of ðæs hālgan reliquium, syle mē.

8. And hē his cyricean getimbrade sēo on āre Scæ Andree þæs apostoles gehālgad is.

9. And hē nele swā micclum swā wē geearniaþ ūs geyrsian.

10. Hē cwæð þæt hē būde on þǽm lande norþweardum wiþ þā Westsǽ.

Chapter 16 Reading Practice

Đā hēt Ælfred Cyng timbran langscipu ongen þā æscas: þā wǽron fulnēah tū swā lange swā þā ōþru; sume hæfdon .lx. āra. sume mā. þā wǽron ǽgþer ge swiftran ge unwealtran, ge ēac hīeran þonne þa ōþru. Nǽron nāwþer ne on Fresisc gescæpene ne on Denisc, būte swā him selfum þūhte þæt hīe nytwyrþoste bēon meahten. Þā æt sumum cirre þæs ilcan gēares cōmon þǽr sex scipu tō Wiht, & þǽr micel yfel gedydon, ǽgþer ge on Defenum ge welhwǽr be þǽm sǽriman. Þā hēt sē cyng faran mid nigonum tō þāra nīwena scipa, & forforon him þone mūþan foran on ūtermere; þā foron hīe mid þrīm scipum ūt ongen hīe, & þrēo stōdon æt ufeweardum þǽm mūþan on drӯgum. Wǽron þā men uppe

on londe of āgāne, þā gefēngon hīe þāra þrēora scipa tū æt
þǣm mūþan ūteweardum, & þā men ofslōgon, & þæt an
oþwand. On þǣm wǣron ēac þā men ofslægene būton
fīfum.

From the *Anglo-Saxon Chronicle* entry for the year 896 :

King Alfred then commanded ships to be built to meet the
Danish fleet: they were nearly twice as long as the other
ships; some had sixty oars, some more. Those were both
swifter and stronger and higher than the others. They were
neither Frisian-shaped or Danish, but as the king himself
thought that they might be most useful. Then, at a particular
occasion in that same year came six [Danish] ships to the
Isle of Wight and there did great evil, both in Devon and
elsewhere by the sea coast. Then the king gave instruction
to travel there with nine of the new ships, and they [Alfred's
ships] got in front of them at the mouth of the river near the
open sea. Then they [the Danes] fared with three ships
against them and three of their ships stood at the upper-end
of the river-mouth on dry ground. Those men were gone up
on the land, and then they [the English] seized two of the
three ships at the entrance to the river-mouth, and slew
those men, and the other ship escaped. In that one all but
five of the men were slain.

17

STRONG VERBS

Strong verbs are verbs in which a **stem vowel** is changed to indicate different tenses.

> ring / rang / rung

is an example of a strong verb in Modern English; the vowel changes from "i" to "a" to "u" depending upon the verb tense.

Although they are not in themselves particularly difficult to understand, strong verbs can cause problems for beginning Old English student translations because the form of a strong verb that you find in a sentence is very often not the form of the verb listed in the dictionary. For example, if you look up the word *sungon* in the dictionary, you won't find it (just as you will not find "sung" in a Modern English dictionary). To find the meaning of *sungon* you must convert the verb to its **infinitive** form, *singan*, which you can then easily find in the dictionary. In order to translate strong verbs, then, we need to be able to recognize the patterns of vowel changes

139

and reconstruct the infinitive from whichever forms we find in sentences.

Conjugating Strong Verbs

To conjugate a strong verb you need to know four pieces of information, the **four principal parts** of the verb:

- The **infinitive**: translated as "to _____." "To read" is the infinitive in the sentence: "Alfred liked <u>to read</u> vernacular books." In Old English the infinitive will end with *an*.

- The 3rd person singular in the past tense, for example, "rang" in the sentence: "He <u>rang</u> the bell." (Note: Many grammar books use the term **preterite** for past tense).

- The **past tense plural**-for example, "sang" in the sentence: "They <u>sang</u> the song." (It is the same for 1st, 2nd, and 3rd person.)

- The **past participle**-for example, "fallen" in "Alfred had <u>fallen</u> on hard times."

For probably 80 percent or more of the strong verbs you'll be translating you won't need the past participle, but it's a good idea to learn it anyway, since it is the principle part from which Modern English forms of Old English strong verbs are drawn. For example, the past participle *tacen* is obviously very similar to Modern English "taken."

There are seven classes of strong verbs. You can use the following poem to help place a verb in its proper class:

The cat will **bite** the bird that will not **fly**
and **spring** upon the mouse when he **comes** by.
He **gives** no quarter and **takes** no guff.
A fool he **holds** him who falls for such stuff.
-- by Patrick W. Conner

Mnemonic tip: memorize the poem.

Taking the Modern English verbs in order from the poem gives us examples, also in order, from the seven Old English strong verb classes:

bite	**bītan**	Class I
fly	**flēon**	Class II
spring	**springan**	Class III
come	**cuman**	Class IV
give	**giefan**	Class V
take	**tacan**	Class VI
hold	**healdan**	Class VII

Unfortunately, different grammar books use different conventions in numbering the verb classes. Some use Roman numerals as we do, but others use Arabic numerals. When in doubt, look at the table of abbreviations that usually appears either at the beginning of the book or the beginning of the book's glossary.

If you learn the principle parts of each of these verbs, you'll know the entire strong verb system. Because strong verb classes are based upon a verb's **vowel** or **diphthong**, you'll be able to match new words with the patterns you've memorized. For example, if you encounter the word *drēogan* ("to endure"), you'll notice that its diphthong *ēo* is the same as the diphthong in *flēon*. You'll then deduce that *drēogan*, like *flēon*, is likely to be a class II strong verb and should therefore follow that particular paradigm.

Class	Infinitive	3rd Person Singular Past	All Plurals Past	Past Participle
I	bītan	bāt	biton	biten
II	flēon	flēah	flugon	flogen
III	springan	sprang	sprungon	sprungen
IV	cuman	cam	cāmon	cumen
V	giefan	geaf	gēafon	giefen
VI	tacan	tōc	tōcon	tacen
VII	healdan	hēold	hēoldon	healden

You can use these principle parts to construct a complete conjugation. Use the 1st conjugation **weak verb** endings, but plug the appropriate strong verb **stems** into the paradigm.

Strong Verb Complete Conjugation Sample:

bītan and singan

Just as in a **weak verb**, the **stem** plus an **ending** creates the **present tense** forms for the various persons.

We'll use *bītan* = "to bite" and *singan* = "to sing" as examples.

First find the **stem** of the verb by removing *an* from the **infinitive**. Removing *an* from *bītan* and *singan* leaves us *bīt* and *sing* as the two **stems**.

Then plug these stems into the paradigm below.

Present Tense

	Ending	Class I	Class III
Singular			
1st Person	e	bīte	singe
2nd Person	est	bītest	singest
3rd Person	eþ	bīteþ	singeþ
Plural			
1st, 2nd and 3rd Persons	oþ or aþ	bītaþ	singaþ

For the 1st and 3rd person singulars in the **past tense** we use the **3rd person singular past**. However, for the 2nd person past tense you must use the vowel of the all plurals past (in this case *i*) with an *e* as the ending.

Past Tense

Singular	Endings	Class I	Class III
1st Person		bāt	sang
2nd Person	e	bite	sunge
3rd Person		bāt	sang
Plural			
1st, 2nd and 3rd Persons	on	biton	sungon

Subjunctive Mood

The **subjunctive mood** uses the **stem** for the **present tense** and the vowel of the **3rd person plural past** for the **past tense**, adding *e* in the singular and *en* in the plural. Thus, the subjunctive past and 2nd person singular past share the same vowel.

Present Tense

	Ending	Class I	Class III
Singular			
1st, 2nd and 3rd Persons	e	bīte	singe
Plural			
1st, 2nd and 3rd Persons	en	bīten	singen

Past Tense

	Ending	Class I	Class III
Singular			
1st, 2nd and 3rd Persons	e	bite	sunge
Plural			
1st, 2nd and 3rd Persons	en	biten	sungen

Imperative Mood

The **imperative mood** uses just the stem for the singular and the stem plus -*að* for the plural. The imperative mood can only be in the 2nd person and only in the present tense.

	Ending	Class I	Class III
Singular			
2nd Person	stem only	bīt	sing
Plural			
2nd Person	að	bītað	singað

Inflected infinitive: **tō bītanne, tō singanne**
Present participle: **bītende, singende**
Past participle: **biten, sungen**

Chapter 17 Vocabulary

Nouns

byrnsweord	flaming sword	(strong, neuter)
cirice	church	(weak, feminine)
ealdor	lord, prince	(strong, masculine)
eard	land	(strong, masculine)
geat	gate	(strong, neuter; accusative plural of *gatu*)
īglond	island	(strong, neuter)
leornere	student	(strong, masculine)
līc	body, corpse	(strong, neuter)
Marīa	Mary	(weak, feminine)
Rōm	Rome	(proper name)
Sancta	Saint	(Latin adjective "holy" used as a noun)
swefn	dream	(strong, neuter)
trēow	pledge	(strong, feminine)
Wendelsǣ	Mediterranean Sea	(feminine; proper name)
world	world	(strong, feminine; often *weoruld*)
wrōht	strife	(strong, feminine)
wyrm	worm, dragon	(strong, masculine)

Strong Verbs

āhebban	to lift, raise, exalt	(Class VI)
becuman	to come, arrive	(Class IV)

gefaran	to travel, go	(Class VI)
fordrīfan	to drive away	(Class I)
forgyldan	to pay for	(Class III)
gehealdan	to keep, preserve	(Class VII)
hēt	commanded	(Class VII)
licgan	to lie	
onginnan	to begin	(Class III)
onwacan	to wake	(Class VI)
gesittan	to settle, remain, sit	
getēon	to draw	(Class II)
tōniman	to open	(Class IV)
ðurh-slēan	to smite through	(Class VI)
weorðan	to become, happen	

Weak Verbs

cirman	to cry out, shout	(1st conjugation)
cohhetan	to bluster, shout	(1st conjugation)
gristbitian	to gnash the teeth	(2nd conjugation)
(ge)nīwian	to renew	(2nd conjugation)
(ge)somnian	to assemble	(2nd conjugation)

Adverbs

ealle	*c* ompletely
feor	far
hider	hither
hlūde	loudly
ðus	thus
ūp	up

Adjectives

an	one	
andweard	present, actual	
ēce	eternal, everlasting	
(ge)lǣrdestan	most learned	
til	good	
ūrne	our	(accusative singular of *ūre*)

Conjunctions

for ðōn	because

Chapter 17 Translation Practice

1. Til bið sē ðe his trēowe gehealdeð.

2. Hē fōr tō Rōme and ðǣr gesæt, ond his līc līð on Sancta Marīan circean.

3. Wearð ðā fordrifen on an īglond ūt on ðǣre Wendelsǣ.

4. And ðonne hē his byrnsweord getȳð and ðās world ealle ðurh-slȳhð.

5. Hī ðā somod ealle ongunnon cohhetan, cirman hlūde ond gristbitian.

6. Gē ealdras tōnymað ðā gatu, and ūp āhebbað ðā ēcan gatu.

7. For ðōn ðū ūs ðus dydest, wē hit ðē forgyldað.

8. Nū gē ðus feor hider on ūrne eard in becōmon.

9. Þā hēt hēo gesomnian ealle þā gelǣrdestan menn and þā leorneras, and him andweardum hēt secgan þæt swefn.

10. Þā sē wyrm onwōc, wrōht wæs genīwad.

Chapter 17 Reading Practice

Ðā ic ðā ðis eall gemunde, ðā gemunde ic ēac hū ic seah ǣr ðǣm ðe hit eall forhergod wǣre ond forbærned, hū ðā ciricean giond eall Angelcynn stōdon māðma ond bōca gefylda, ond ēac micel mengeo Godes ðīowa. Ond ðā swīðe lȳtle fiorme ðāra bōca wiston, for ðǣm ðe hīe hiora nānwuht ongiotan ne meahton, for ðǣm ðe hīe nǣron on hiora āgen geðīode āwritene. Swelce hīe cwǣden: "Ūre ieldran, ðā ðe ðās stōwa ǣr hīoldon, hīe lufodon wīsdōm, ond ðurh ðone hīe begēaton welan, ond ūs lǣfdon. Hēr mon mæg gīet gesīon hiora swæð, ac wē him ne cunnon æfter spyrigean."

From King Alfred's prose preface to his translation of Gregory the Great's *Pastoral Care*

When I remembered all this, I remembered how I saw, before it was all destroyed and burned, how the churches around all of England stood filled with treasures and books, and also with a great multitude of the servants of God. And those received very little benefit from those books, because they were not able to understand them, because they were not written in their own language. It is as if they said, "Our ancestors, who previously held this place, they loved wisdom, and through it they obtained wealth, and left it to us. Here one may still see their track, but we may not follow after them."

18

PRETERITE-PRESENT VERBS

A few Old English verbs (unfortunately they are important and rather common) combine features of **strong verbs** and **weak verbs**. These verbs take what would normally be a strong verb past tense (also called a **preterite**) and transfer it to the present. They then build a **weak verb paradigm** upon that strong verb present tense.

This sounds confusing, but makes sense when you see it applied to an actual verb. The basic idea is that *preterite-present verbs are strong verbs that have their past tenses and present tenses swapped*. This is why they are called "preterite-present."

Preterite-present verbs are often used as **modals**; they are combined with other verbs (usually those other verbs are in the **infinitive** form) to produce constructions like "to remember to go" or "to dare to fight."

The important verbs in this category are:

āgan	to possess
cunnan	to know how to
dugan	to achieve
durran	to dare
magan	to be able to
mōtan	to be allowed to
munan	to remember
sculan	must, to be obligated
ðurfan	to need
unnan	to grant
witan	to know something

> **Note:** You'll be seeing these verbs a lot, so you might as well memorize them now.

Conjugating Preterite-Present Verbs

To construct a conjugation for a preterite-present verb, do the following:

Subtract the -*an* ending from the **infinitive**. This gives you the **stem** of the verb:

> *witan -an = wit*

Use the strong verb paradigm to determine what the past singular would be.

Wit would be a Class I strong verb, so, following the Class I strong verb paradigm, we determine that the past tense would be *wāt*. This now becomes the **stem** for the paradigm, and what you would have expected to be the present tense (*wit*, which, remember, is the stem minus the *an* ending of the infinitive) moves to the past tense.

Here is a diagram of the process:

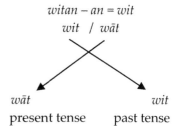

apply strong verb stem vowel change:

move strong past to present tense:

move stem to past tense:

Preterite-Present Verbs Paradigm: Examples

Present Tense

Singular	
1st Person	**wāt**
2nd Person	**wāst**
3rd Person	**wāt**
Plural	
1st, 2nd and 3rd Persons	**witon**

Note: the present plural forms use the same root vowel as the infinitive.

Past Tense

Singular	
1st, 2nd and 3rd Persons	**wiste** or **wisse**
Plural	
1st, 2nd and 3rd Persons	**wiste** or **wisse**

Chapter 18 Vocabulary

Nouns

būtū	both	(strong, neuter)
dæg	day	(strong, masculine)
ēa	river	(strong, feminine)
morgen	morning	(radical consonant, masculine)
nēdþearf	need	(strong, feminine)
sige	victory	(strong, feminine)
sylf	self	(strong and weak)
unfriþ	un-peace, hostility	(strong, masculine)

Verbs

āgan	to possess, control	(preterite-present)
cierran	to turn	(weak, 1st conjugation)
(ge)flīeman	put to flight	(weak, 1st conjugation)
(ge)hīeran	to hear	(weak, 1st conjugation)
(ge)munan	to remember	(preterite-present)
ofslēan	to slay	(strong, Class VI)
siglan	to sail	(weak, 1st conjugation)
(ge)ðencan	to think	(weak, 1st conjugation)

Adverbs

beæftan	after
forþ	forth

Adjectives

longe	long
mycel	large, great

Chapter 18 Translation Practice

1. Hwæt sceal ic singan?

2. Þā on morgenne gehīerdun þæt þæs cyninges þegnas, þe him beæftan wærun, þæt sē cyning ofslægen wæs.

3. Ond hīe būtū geflīemdon ond longe on dæg sige āhton.

4. And ūs is mycel nēdþearf þæt wē ūs sylfe geðencean and gemunan.

5. Þā cirdon hīe ūp on ðā ēa, for þǣm hīe nō dorston forþ bi þǣre ēa siglan for unfriþe.

Chapter 18 Reading Practice

Ðā gemunde ic hū sīo ǣ wæs ǣrest on Ebreisc-geðīode funden, ond eft, ðā hīe Crēacas geliornodon, ðā wendon hīe hīe on hiora āgen geðīode ealle, ond ēac ealle ōðre bēc. Ond eft Lǣdenware swǣ same, siððan hīe hīe geliornodon, hīe hīe wendon ealla ðurh wīse wealhstodas on hiora āgan geðīode. Ond ēac ealla ōðra Crīstna ðīoda sumne dæl hiora on hiora āgen geðīode wendon. Forðȳ mē ðyncð betre, gif īow swǣ ðyncð, ðæt wē ēac suma bēc, ðā ðe nīedbeðearfosta sīen eallum monnum tō wiotonne, ðæt wē ðā on ðæt geðīode wenden ðe wē ealle gecnāwan mægen, ond gedōn swǣ wē swīðe ēaðe magon mid Godes fultume, gif wē ðā stilnesse habbað, ðætte eall sīo gioguð ðe nū is on Angelcynne frīora monna, ðāra ðe ðā spēda hæbben ðæt hīe ðǣm befēolan mægen, sīen tō liornunga oðfæste (ðā hwīle ðe hīe tō nānre ōðerre note ne mægen) oð ðone first ðe hīe wel cunnen Englisc gewrite ārǣdan.

From King Alfred's prose preface to his translation of Gregory the Great's *Pastoral Care*

Then I remembered how the law was first founded in the Hebrew-language, and afterward, when the Greeks learned it, then they themselves turned it into their own language and all other books. And afterwards the Latin-dwellers (Romans) the same, after they had learned them, they turned them all through wise translators into their own language. And also all the other Christian peoples turned some portion of theirs into their own language. Therefore to me it seems better, if it seems so to you, that we also turn certain books, those which are most necessary for all men to know, into that language which we all may understand, and also do so as quickly as we may with God's help, if we have peace enough, so that all that young free-born men now in England, those who are able to do so, may be set to learning (as long as they are not needed in some other work) until they can well read English writing with understanding.

19

TRANSLATING TRICKS

Now that you have mastered the fundamentals of Old English grammar, you are ready to learn a few tricks for translating that will make your task easier.

Modal plus infinitive

The modal plus infinitive combination is very common in Old English poetry. Remember that a modal is a helping verb such as "could," "would," "should" or "must." While in Modern English a modal would be followed by a verb in the correct number for the subject ("I should go to the store"), Old English speakers would use an infinitive ("I should to go to the store"). Remember that the infinitive ends in *-an* or *-ian*.

Once you can recognize the modal plus infinitive construction, you'll start seeing it everywhere in Old English poetry:

> *Nu wē **sculan** <u>herian</u>* ("Now we **must** <u>to praise</u>" = "Now we **must** <u>praise</u>").

The **modal** and the <u>infinitive</u> can be in either **modal** + <u>infinitive</u> or <u>infinitive</u> + **modal** order:

> *Ic swefna cyst <u>secgan</u> **wille*** ("I <u>to tell</u> **wish** of the greatest of dreams" = "I wish to tell of the greatest of dreams").

The **modal** and the <u>infinitive</u> do not always need to be next to each other in the sentence:

> ***Mæg*** *ic be mē selfum sōþ-giedd <u>wrecan</u>* ("I **can** about myself a true song <u>to sing</u> " = "I can sing a true song about myself").

Partitive genitive

The **partitive genitive** is a construction used to indicate one or more things which are a subset of a larger group. We still use the partitive genitive in Modern English in phrases such as "five of them" in the sentence "Five <u>of them</u> approached the king," but we would find the phrase "Seven <u>of people</u> approached the king" to be ungrammatical. In Old English, however, the equivalent of "five of people" would be perfectly idiomatic. Thus we get sentences like:

> *Þǣr wæs <u>mādma</u> fela* ("There was many <u>of treasures</u>" = "There were many treasures")

> *Fela þǣr wæs <u>wera</u> ond <u>wīfa</u>* ("There was many <u>of men</u> and <u>of women</u>" = "There were many men and women").

Note that the word *fela* ("many") is used very frequently with partitive genitive nouns.

Tips for the dative case

- When in doubt, translate the dative case as "with." A fairly high percentage of dative-case nouns that you encounter can be translated as "with + noun." "With" also works for most translations of instrumentals.

- **The locative dative**: in Chapter 6: Word Order and Cases, we discussed the ways the **dative** can be translated using Modern English **prepositions**. We also noted, in our discussion of the **accusative** case, that the accusative can be used to indicate "motion towards" something. The dative case is often used to indicate a location (hence "locative") with the idea of something being *stationary* rather than moving. You will almost always get this sense of the dative correct by translating with "in," or "on," but it can sometimes help to remember that a dative without a preposition may simply be indicating location. Thus in the sentence *Þær æt hȳðe stōd hringedstefna* ("There at the harbor stood the ring-prowed ship"), *hȳðe* is dative singular because the ship is not moving.

- *-um* is your friend. The dative plural ending *-um* is one of the few near-constants in Old English. When you see *um*, it's nearly always dative and usually dative plural.

The "ge" prefix

Many **verbs** have the prefix *ge* appended to them. *Ge* often indicates a perfective form of a verb (something that has been done once and is finished) and is frequently found when the past participle is used.

You will notice the prefix *ge* when you are looking up verbs in a glossary or dictionary. Usually the dictionary lists the verb alphabetically under the **infinitive** without including the *ge* prefix. Thus *geþolian* would be listed under *þolian* and *gemanian* under*manian*. Words that take a *ge* prefix may be listed in a form like *(ge) þolian* but nevertheless alphabetized under *þolian*. But a few dictionaries will alphabetize some verbs with *ge* prefixes under *ge* (usually this incredibly annoying practice is only done with the few verbs that always take a *ge* prefix).

Thus when looking up a verb in the dictionary you should first subtract the *ge* prefix and search for the **infinitive**. If you can't find it, then look under the *ge*-prefixed spelling. Interestingly, words with other prefixes, such as *for, un* and *a*, are listed alphabetically under their prefixed form.

There is the additional confusion that, as we discussed in Chapter 13, some **nouns** can take a *ge* prefix as well. This usually occurs in the plural and indicates some sort of jointness or togetherness about the noun: *gebrōþru* ("brothers"). Again, your best bet is mentally to delete the *ge* and look up the root of the word first, only searching for the "ge" form if you don't find a root.

Things that start with Thorn and Eth

One of the challenges about learning Old English is the unfamiliar writing system, and the most unfamiliar parts are the letters thorn (Þ þ) and eth (Ð ð).

First, remember that in Old English þ and ð are completely interchangeable (as are their capital-letter forms, Þ and Ð). All of them simply indicate the interdental fricative sound that we indicate with the digraph "th".

The next problem is that there are a variety of short words beginning with thorn and eth that are very important for Old English grammar. These words, because they are all short and all start with the unfamiliar letters, are often easily confused. So there they are:

The worst offender: Ða a.k.a. Þa, þa and ða

þa can mean a variety of things. On its own it means "then" or "when" and often appears at the beginning of a sentence (which is why this form is one of the ones that most frequently uses the capital letter spelling Ða).

þa is also a singular, feminine, accusative demonstrative pronoun, which mean, roughly "to that [female thing]."

More commonly, þa is a plural demonstrative pronoun in either the nominative or the accusative and so equivalent to "those."

To review:

Þā can be an **adverb** that means "when" or "then." *Þā* can also be a plural **demonstrative pronoun** in the nominative or accusative cases (meaning "those" or "to those"). It can also be a singular feminine demonstrative pronoun in the accusative case. *Þā* can also be part of the idiomatic expression, *for þā þe,* which, like *for þām þe,* means "because." Use other information in the sentence (for example, the case and gender of the noun to which *þā* is attached) to help you determine which form of *þā* is being used in a given sentence. Also, when you come across *"Đā þā,"* you can almost always translate it as "then, when."

Second worst: Þam a.k.a. Đam, ðam, þam

"þam means dative" is a simple rule of thumb that usually works. þam is the dative case singular demonstrative pronoun for both masculine and neuter things. It is also the dative plural for all genders.

But, you'll also see þam show up in the idiomatic expression "for þam þe" which means "because."

Third worst: þe a.k.a. Đe, ðe, Þe

ðe is the relative particle generally translated as "which" (though it can be "who" or "whom" when referring to a person). It does not change based on case or number, which makes it easy to memorize but makes translating more difficult.

Often þe is paired with a demonstrative (like ða) to indicate case and number. So "ða þe" means "with those which" and "se ðe" means "he who."

þe is also part of the idiomatic expression "for þam þe" or "for þara þe" (i.e., the formula is "for X þe" where X is a demonstrative pronoun. This always can be translated simply as "because."

Other short þ words:

þu : thou, you

þin : thine, yours

þis : this (various inflected forms þises, þeos, þisse and þissum)

þæ s: genitive singular of se or þæt, it means "of that."

þara : genitive plural for all genders, means "of those"

þy : instrumental for "that", means "with that," "by means of that"

A few common idioms

It is best simply to memorize that *for þām þe* in its various inflected forms (see above under *Þā*) means "because." Here are a few other common Old English expressions:

- *swā swā* looks like it would be "so so" or "as as," but the best translation is probably "just as" or "such as."

- *swylce* means "such," but it very often can be translated at "likewise."

- *samod ætgædere* appears to be redundant (together together), but should just be taken as a very emphatic "together."

Steps for finding the infinitive of a strong verb

1). Is there a simple ending of -est -eþ or -aþ?

> YES: The word is a present tense verb. Delete that ending and add -an and you've got the infinitive.

> NO: Go to step 2.

2). Does the verb end in -on?

> YES: Then the word is an all-plurals past and we're going to need to work through the vowel change. Look up the vowel or diphthong in the table to determine the class of the verb (unfortunately a **u** can be class III or class IV). Then look across to the appropriate stem vowel. Put that vowel in place of the one in the -on form, switch the -on to -an, and you've got the infinitive.

> NO: Go to step 3

3). Does the verb have no ending? (i.e., it ends in a consonant).

> YES: It is a past tense, either in the first or third person. Look up the vowel or diphthong in the table to determine the class. Then look across to the appropriate stem vowel. Replace the vowel you already have with the vowel from the table and add -an.

> NO: Go to step 4

4). Does the verb end in -e or -en?

> NO: You may have missed something or the word you are looking at may not be a verb. Now is the time to look up what you have in a dictionary.

> YES: Here's where the fun begins. The verb could be a past participle. It could also be a past tense in the second person,

a present tense in the first person, or a subjunctive in first, second or third persons in the present tense (yes, not very helpful).

5). If the verb ends in -e:

Find the subject of the verb in the sentence.

Is the subject first person singular (ic)?

YES: Delete the -e from the word, add -an and you have the infinitive.

NO: Is the subject 2nd person (ge, þu) ?

YES: You will need to look up the vowel in the table under "3rd person singular past". Then find the infinitive. Replace the vowel you have with the one in the infinitive. Delete -e. Add -an.

NO: Then you probably have a subjunctive form, which means that you will not be able to tell the tense. Nevertheless, you can still find the infinitive. Look up the vowel in the table under "3rd person singular past," then find the infinitive. Replace the vowel you have with the one in the infinitive. Delete -e. Add -an.

6). If the verb ends in -en: It can either be a past participle or a plural subjunctive in either the present or past tenses. Unfortunately, these forms will look exactly the same. The good news is that if you find one in the participle column of the table, you can trace back the vowel and create the correct infinitive without too much trouble (i.e., change the stem vowel, delete -en and then add -ad).

[N.B.: Please trust me that this gets *much* easier when you are translating in context]

Class	infinitive	3rd per past	all plurals past	participle
I	ī	ā	i (+on)	i (+en)
II	ēo	ēa	u (+on)	o (+en)
	ū			
III	i	a	u (+on)	u (+en) [ring, rang, rung]
IV	e	æ	ǣ (+on)	o (+en)
	u	a	ā (+0n)	u (+en) [come, came]
V	e	ea	ēa (+on)	e (+en) [give, gave]
VI	a	ō	ō (+on)	a (+en)
VII	ǣ	ē	ē (+on)	ǣ (+en)

When you get stuck

There will be times when you simply get stuck translating. Here are a few tips for getting through these blocks.

- Look at the **cases** of nouns and pronouns, particularly **demonstrative** pronouns. Make sure that you have construed them correctly.

- If you can't find something in the dictionary, guess that it may be a **strong verb** and reconstruct its **infinitive** form.

- Look for the verb at the end of the sentence (this is particularly common when translating poetry).

- Although it seems like a good idea simply to look up every unfamiliar word in the sentence and provide an interlinear translation, it is very often more useful to figure out how the sentence works grammatically and *then* plug in the vocabulary.

- Go back over any relative clauses and make sure that you've construed them properly-have you accidentally translated *þe* as "the"? Remember that in a relative clause *þe* means "which" and re-translate accordingly.

20

CONCLUSION: WHAT NEXT?

Congratulations on completing *Drout's Quick and Easy Old English*. If you've mastered the material in this book you are well on your way to being able to read some of the best literature in existence. Your next step should be to read and translate some of that literature. We say "read and translate" because even at this early stage there is much Old English that you can probably just read. Ælfric, abbot of Eynsham, is perhaps the greatest prose writer of Old English, and he wrote often so clearly and simply that you should be able to understand much of his work without great difficulty.

Poetry is both more difficult and more rewarding. At first, you probably will not be able to read poetry immediately the way you can read prose, but you should be readily able to translate poetry with a dictionary in hand. The best practice is to write a **gloss** for the poem, writing the Modern English equivalent of a word over the Old English word as you translate. We recommend that you also note parts of speech, cases or verb tenses, particularly when you are not entirely certain about a sentence's meaning.

> Adv   subj subj gen. pl.
> Here Athelstan King, of earls lord
> Her Æþelstan cyning, eorla dryhten
>
> gen. pl.
> of rings giver) and his brother also
> beorna beahgifa, and his broþor eac
>
> accus. = direct object
> Edmund atheling, life-long glory
> Eadmund ætheling, ealdorlangne tir
>
> d. sing.   gen.pl. dat. pl.
> won/defeated at battle   of swords with edges
> geslogon æt sæcce, sweorda ecgum
>
> around Brunanburg.
> ymbe Brunanburh.
>
> Here king Athelstan, the lord of earls, giver of rings,
> and his brother also, Edmund atheling, won, with the
> edges of swords, lifelong glory in battle around
> Brunanburg.

If you make a special effort to understand the grammar of the sentences you are translating, you will soon be able to appreciate the beauty and power of Old English poetry. We recommend that you begin with some of the simpler poems such as "The Battle of Brunanburh" or some poems from the *Exeter Book* , perhaps "The Fortunes of Men," "The Panther," and "The Whale." When you have more of a grasp on Old English poetic syntax, move on to the much-loved "elegies," including "The Wanderer," "The Seafarer," and "The Wife's Lament."

When you have a firm grasp of Old English poetic translation, it is time to tackle the greatest and most famous of Old English poems, *Beowulf*. The syntax and vocabulary of *Beowulf* can be difficult, but

Beowulf is a great poem and well worth the effort it may take to translate and read it.

We'll also remind you again that *Drout's Quick and Easy Old English* is a simplified introduction to Old English. If you become more serious about Old English, you will need to use a fully developed, detailed grammar. The standard grammar now available is:

Bruce Mitchell and Fred C. Robinson. *A Guide to Old English*. Oxford: Blackwell, 1994.

Frederic G. Cassidy and Richard N. Ringler. *Bright's Old English Grammar and Reader*, 3rd ed. New York: Holt, Rinehart and Winson, 1971 is now sadly out of print, but used copies can be found. *Bright's* reader is extremely useful.

The most comprehensive guide to Old English grammar is A. Campbell. *Old English Grammar*. Oxford: Oxford University Press, 1959 (repr. 1968).

Also useful is Richard Marsden. *The Cambridge Old English Reader*. Cambridge: Cambridge University Press, 2004.

But whether or not you decide to pursue Old English further, we suggest that you take a moment here to congratulate yourself on making a good beginning towards knowing "those things that are most important for people to know." We think King Alfred would be pleased with your effort.

APPENDIX ON SOUND CHANGES

Languages change. The pronunciation of individual vowels and consonants, the meanings of individual words, even the very rules of grammar are subject to change over time. Philologists and linguists have discovered that there are patterns to these changes, that they follow regular and logical rules. The study of such changes and of how we pronounce words is called **phonology**. In this appendix we will discuss the most important phonological changes in the history of Old and Modern English.

Old English and Modern English are part of the Germanic branch of the larger Indo-European language family. A simplified representation of the evolution of Old English from primitive Indo-European and Germanic is given below:

> Indo-European → Germanic → West Germanic → Low West Germanic → Old English

The people who spoke Germanic did not use writing, so our knowledge of this language comes entirely from the study of the later, differentiated languages. As English is the oldest written European vernacular, a very detailed record of spelling changes is available to us; in turn, these spelling changes mark pronunciation changes. From the written records we are able to reconstruct what brought about these shifts and how words sounded before and after them. In this chapter we will consider changes in the Germanic precursors to Old English words, that is, what came before and led to Old English sounds and spellings being written down the way they are. For convenience, all Germanic forms (or proto-Old English forms) will be marked by an asterisk (*) and shifts will be marked by an arrow (→). All Old English words will be in *italics*.

The most general change over time is that <u>vowel sounds shift forward and upward</u>. Recall the difference between **back** vowels and **front** vowels: we say Old English $\bar{a}$ / $\bar{o}$ / $\bar{u}$ in the back of our mouths; we say Old English $\bar{æ}$ / $\bar{e}$ / $\bar{i}$ in the front. In turn, those two sets of vowels work from **lower** to **upper**: we say $\bar{a}$ lower in the mouth than $\bar{u}$, and $\bar{æ}$ lower than $\bar{i}$. The corollary to that overall vowel shift is that high and front vowels tend to draw low and back vowels towards them: an $\bar{i}$ sound in a word will tend to cause other vowels in the word to become higher and more towards the front of the mouth.

We will discuss six major sound changes relevant to Old English. In the chronological order they occur in the evolution of *Germanic to Old English they are: **gemination**, a → o, **fronting** of a → æ, **breaking**, **diphthongization** after initial palatal, and the most important, **i-mutation**. We will close our discussion by looking at the sound changes described by **Grimm's Law** (and the exceptions to these changes, which are described by **Verner's Law**). The two laws explain why we say 'frozen' when King Alfred wrote *froren*.

Note that a word can-and usually will-undergo more than one sound change on its way to Old English.

1. Gemination

From the Latin word for twins, *gemini*, this term explains how some double or 'twinned' consonants come about.

<u>A short vowel</u> + <u>a single consonant</u> + **j** will lead to a lengthening of that inbetween (or **medial**) consonant; to spell this lengthening, the letter will double. Last, the **j** will tend to fall out.

> *bedjan → *beddjan → *biddan* [gemination; i-mutation]
> *saljan → *salljan → *sellan* [gemination; i-mutation]

The consonants **f** and **g** will geminate as **bb** and **cg** respectively. However, if the word has a long vowel or the semi-vowel **r**, gemination is prevented.

> *hafjan → *habbjan → *habban* [gemination]
> *segjan → *secgjan → *secgan* [gemination]

But:

> *sandjan, *sōcjan, and *nærjan will **not** undergo
> gemination. Note their Old English forms: *sendan, sēcan,*
> *nerian.*

Gemination is important to recognize because some Old English verbs, such as *habban* and *secgan*, have infinitives that are geminated but some conjugated forms that are not:

> infinitive *habban secgan*
> pres. 3 sg *hafað segð*

This difference is explained by the **absorption** of **j** in the *Gmc conjugation for the 3rd person singular before the consonant could be geminated. The **j** disappears before gemination can take place:

infinitive *framjan → *frammjan → *fremman* [gemination; i-mutation]

pres. 3 sg *framjiþ → *framiþ → *fremeþ* [absorption of **j** ; i-mutation]

2. The Change of a to o

This sound change explains why a Modern German speaker says "gans" and we say "goose,", and why Old English texts feature both *lamb* and *lomb, ond* and *and.*

In the proto-Old English stage, the sound of the vowel **a**, before a **nasal** consonant (**m** or **n**), tended to change to a sound best spelled by **o**. This effect of this change was most noticeable in the earlier period of the West Saxon dialect (EWS)-exactly the time and place King Alfred was writing.

> *lamb → lomb *and → ond *manig → monig*

However, in the later period of the West-Saxon dialect (LWS), these 'o' forms had often reverted back to their original 'a' forms. Thus you will see both.

A corollary to this change is that before certain letters (the 'voiceless-spirants **h**, **f**, **þ**, **s**) the cluster **on** underwent further change: the nasal **n** dropped out and the vowel **o** was **lengthened** as a consequence. Hence we now say "soft" and "goose," whereas the modern German retains "sanft" and "gans":

> *sanft → *sonft → *sōft* [a → o; lengthening]
> *gans → *gons → *gōs* [a → o; lengthening]

Under the same conditions, ***in** and ***un** become *ī* and *ū* : compare the evolution of the word "five," from *finf to Old English *fīf* and to Modern German "'fünf," where the **n** is still present.

3. Fronting of a to æ

When *Germanic **a** was not changing to **o** before a nasal, it tended to move to the sound **æ** at the front of the mouth:

sad, heavy	*sad → *sæd*
back	*bac→ *bæc*
noble	*aÐele → *æÐele*
skillful	*craftig→ *cræftig*

Note that Modern English reclaims the **a** spelling in "sad" and "back" but keeps the **æ** pronunciation; this is one example why spelling is more phonetic in Old English than in Modern.

This **fronting** would occur unless other **back** sounds (notably **w** and the back vowels **a**, **o**, **u**) worked in a second syllable to counteract this shift:

day	*dag→ *dæg*
day [gen. sg.]	*dages→ *dæges*
day [nom. pl.]	*dagas→ *dagas*

Note that with respect to declension, this shift renders the **base** of the noun "day" into mixed forms. If the inflectional ending has a back vowel, here an "a" in the nominative plural, the **a** of the first syllable will not shift to **æ**. But if the inflectional ending has an 'e', as in the genitive singular, there is nothing to counteract the shift.

4. Breaking

This term explains a cluster of sound changes from single vowels (monothongs) to double vowels (diphthongs). What happens is that before certain consonants and consonant pairs a single **front**

vowel will "break" and be spelled as a double. The rules for this **breaking** are fairly complex but the principle is always the same: the sound of a vowel in the earlier part of a word will be changed by the force of a particular consonant or consonant pair that follows. It is easier to show than explain:

1	æ → **ea**	before **h, l** + cons., **r** + cons.
eight	*æhta → *eahta*	**h**
half	*hælf → *healf*	**l** + cons.
warm	*wærm → *wearm*	**r** + cons.

Note that in the case of "half" and "warm," Modern English reverts back to spelling with a monothong even as the diphthong sound is retained. We don't say 'half' with a low **a** sound; nor do we say it with an **æ** sound (though readers in Boston might protest.) In this way Modern English sounds right but spells wrong, obscuring the diphthong sound of the broken vowel even though the **lf** sound has forced the **æ** to roll into **ea**. Note also that the examples above have gone through **fronting** and then **breaking**: *warm → *wærm → *wearm*.

2	e → **eo**	before **h, lc, lh, r** + cons.
to fight	*fehtan → *feohtan*	**h**
money	*feh → *feoh*	**h**
to milk	melcan → *meolcan*	**lc**
seal	*selh → *seolh*	**lh**
to help	helpan → *helpan*	**no breaking**
heart	herte → *heorte*	**r**
earth	*erþe → *eorþe*	**r**

Note that breaking of "e" before "l" is **limited** to **lc** and **lh**; breaking does not occur in the infinitive *helpan,* or in other **l + consonant**' clusters such as *swelgan,* "to swallow," or *sweltan,* "to die." A notable exception is the pret. 3 sg. *healp.*

3	**i → io**	before **h, r** + cons.
to arrange	*tihhian → *tiohhian*	**h**
herdsman	*hirdi → *hiordi → *hierde*	[breaking; i-mutation]

Breaking of **i → io** is very rare.

4	**vowels**	before **h**
light	*līht → *līoht* (often *lēoht*)	**ī + h → īo**
near, about	*nǣh → *nēah*	**ǣ + h → ēa**

Breaking of long vowels is also uncommon.

Breaking is important to recognize because it helps explain some discrepancies between spelling and pronunciation in both Old English and Modern English; it also is an important feature of several verb classes, where the forms of the verb are variable depending on whether or not the conditions for breaking are met. The **four principal parts** of Class IIIb **strong verbs** will serve as examples:

	infinitive	pret 3 sg.	pret 3 pl.	past part.	
	e → eo	**æ → ea**	**u**	**o**	
save, defend	*beorgan*	*bearg*	*burgon*	*borgen*	**r** + cons.
cut	*ceorfan*	*cearf*	*curfon*	*corfen*	**r** + cons.
fight	*feohtan*	*feaht*	*fuhton*	*fohten*	**h**

Breaking is limited the first two principal parts since the back vowels **u** and **o** do not break. Another verb where breaking is important is *sēon*, to see:

> Vc *sehan → *seohan → *sēon* [breaking; loss of medial 'h' lengthens 'eo' to 'ēo']

Because **breaking** is caused by a complex set of vowels and consonants in coordination, it is better to work backwards to see if any particular diphthong will have been brought about by local conditions rather than try to memorize all these pairings.

5. Diphthongization after initial palatals c, g, sc

In which one of the simplest sound changes gets the most ungainly name. This is why you sh**ear** a sh**eep** and eat its ch**ee**se.

A **palatal** is a s**oft** consonant sound made at the roof of the mouth (such as the **y** sound in "yes") while a **velar** is a h**ard** , more guttaral, consonant sound (such as the **k** in "king.") Palatal **c** and **g** come before **front** vowels, while the velar **c** and **g** sounds come before **back vowels**:

Palatal	Velar
dīc [ditch]	*caru* [care]
cealf [calf]	*hōc* [hook]
gīet [yet]	*gold* [gold]
fæger [fair]	*gān* [to go]
dæg [day]	*dagas* [days]

If a word starts with a palatal **c** or **g**, or with the palatal cluster **sc**, some single front vowels will change to double vowels, that is, they will become **diphthongs**. The effect is just like **breaking**, except that the element responsible for the shift comes before the vowel:

1. **æ → ea**   *cæster → *ceaster*   [town, castle]

                *scæl → *sceal*   [shall]

2. **ǣ → ēa**   *scǣp → *scēap*   [sheep]

                *gǣr → *gēar*   [year]

3. **e → ie**   *gefan → *giefan*   [to give]

                *sceran → *scieran*   [to shear]

Each of the three vowel shifts can be caused by each of the palatals. Note that in Modern English some of these diphthongs remain (though changed) and some have reverted to monothong spellings. The word 'cheese' provides us with a rather strong example of sound change:

> *Lat.* cāseus → *cǣsi → *cēasi → OE *cīese* → MidE chese → MnE 'cheese'

Here the Latin word has been borrowed into *Germanic, where the stem vowel 'ǣ' has been palatalized to 'ēa' and then raised in Old English by **i-mutation** to 'īe'; next, the palatal 'c' has been made transparent by the 'ch' in Middle English; finally, the diphthong sound 'īe', obscured in the Middle English spelling, has been been spelled out with the doubled 'ee'. Say cheese.

6. I-Mutation

This is the most important and influential cluster of sound changes relevant to our study of Old English and it exemplifies the general principle stated at the beginning of this chapter that English <u>vowel sounds tend to shift forward and upward over time</u>.

The most forceful mechanism in Old English of that general shift is that vowels are drawn to the front and top of the mouth by the following presence of an *i, ī, or j* in the same word; this process, **i-mutation**, works by **assimilation** since other vowels are changed in nature (mutated) so as to more closely resemble the sounds of *i* and *ī*. (Recall that the Modern English pronunciation of "i" is not correct for Old English; the OE sound of *ī* is properly e "e" as in "tee-hee," "i" as it is pronounced in the French alphabet).

At times, it seems that **i-mutation**, or **i-umlaut** as it is also called, affects every single vowel in Old English - but don't worry, because this is a consistent change that still makes sense in Modern English. Hence, this sound change helps explain we say one "mouse" and two "mice," one "man" and two "men," and many other seeming incongruities. **Umlaut** is the equivalent German term given to the raising of a vowel sound by the sound of "i."

How it works

Under the strong phonological influence of **i-mutation**, almost all vowels can be drawn higher and forward by the presence of *i, ī,* or *j* in the <u>following syllable</u>. (The semi-vowel *j* carries the quality of "y" in Modern English "yes.") **Back vowels** become fronted and **low front vowels** become raised as a speaker anticipates the higher vowel sound coming in the next syllable. After i-mutation, the *i, ī,* or *j* tends to fall out or remain as an *e*.

Short	1. æ → e	*mæti → *mete*	[meat]
Vowels	2. a, o + m/n → e	*wandian → *wendan*	[to turn]
	3. o → e	*dohtri → *dehter*	[daughter]
	4. u → y	*cuning → *cyning*	[king]
Long	5. ā → ǣ	*hāljan → *hǣlan*	[to heal]
Vowels	6. ō → ē	*dōmjan → *dēman*	[to judge]
	7. ū → ȳ	*mūsi → *mȳs*	[mice]
Diphthongs	8. ea, eo, io → ie	*ealdira → *ieldra*	[older]
	9. ēa, ēo, īo → īe	*frīondi → *frīend*	[friend]

Note that many of these shifts help explain irregular plurals and mixed forms in Modern English. "One mouse," "two mice" is now clear, and we can also see how "doom" and "deem" are related, as are, by analogy to OE *dehter,* the mixed forms "brother" (originally *brōðor*) and "brethren" (where an "i" has fallen out between "h" and "r"). We can also see how some words have vowels which have risen more than once, as for example "to heal": first *hāljan,* then OE *hǽlan,* then finally, Modern English "heal," which has the highest vowel sound of the three.

Resolution of I-Mutation

1. After i-mutation, the semi-vowel **j** will fall out, unless it comes after **r** preceded by a **short** vowel, where it will then remain as **i**:

	nærjan → nerian	[to save, to preserve]
	færjan → ferian	[to carry]
But :	*lārjan → lǽran*	[to teach]
	fremman → fremman	[to achieve]

After i-mutation, a final unstressed ī will fall out if preceded by a long syllable; it becomes an **e** if preceded by a short syllable:

long	*dāli → *dǽli → dǽl*	[a portion]
short	*slǽgi → slegi → slege*	[a hit or blow]

After i-mutation, a medial **i** becomes an "e," except when followed by **c, g, sc, ng,** where it remains as **i**:

*morgin → *mergin → mergen* [morning]

hǽfig → hefig [heavy; severe]

2. In Late West-Saxon (LWS), the diphthongs *ie* and *īe* tended to **resolve**, or simplify, into the single vowels *i* / *y* and *ī* / *ȳ*, as in the following:

*hiordi → hierde → hyrde	[io → ie → y]
*gelēafjan → gelīefan → gelīfan	[ēa → īe → ī]

In *gelīfan*, the assimilation to the high *ī* sound is in full evidence as the low front diphthong 'ēa' has been mutated into the high front monthong *ī* ; note, however, that the **length** of the vowel has been conserved.

Further Importance of I-Mutation

It is hard to underestimate the scope and importance of i-mutation in the development of Old English words, not least because the vowel shifts brought about by this process are the source of many initial difficulties and sudden illuminations in learning Old English. We have already discussed the importance of i-mutation for the declension of some minor nouns, such as *ān fōt, twēgen fēt*; we should now also know why the dative singular of *brōðor* is *brēðer*, and likewise can guess at the relation between "strong" and "strength," and "foul" and "filth."

Further, i-mutation is extremely prevalent in the formation of whole verb families, particularly 1st conjugation weak verbs. These tend to be formed from nouns or adjectives that have been turned into verbs by the addition of **jan**; with this suffix marking the infinitive, the conditions for i-mutation are set:

noun	(food) + *jan → fēdan*	to feed
noun	*weorc* (work) + *jan → wyrcan*	to work
adjective	*hāl* (whole) + *jan → hǣlan*	to heal
pret. sg.	*dranc* (drank) + *jan → drencan*	to drench

There are dozens of further examples of such synthetic formation of verbs from nouns, adjectives and even other verbs, in particular the preterite singular of strong verbs as with *dranc* and *drencan*.

Last, i-mutation plays in important role in creating twin or variant stem-vowel forms for the 2nd and 3rd person present tense of verbs such as *healdan*, "to hold or rule" and *fōn*, "to seize" (both Class VII):

infinitive	*healdan*	
pres. 2 sg.	*healdest* or **hieltst**	(**i-mutation**; loss of "e")
pres. 3 sg.	*healdeð* or **hielt**	(**i-mutation**; loss of "e"; assimilation of "ð" to "t")
infinitive	**fohan → fōn*	("o" does not break; loss of medial "h"; contraction)
pres. 2 sg.	**fōhist →fēhst*	(i-mutation; "e" drops out before loss of medial "h" can occur)
pres. 3 sg.	**fōhið → fēhð*	(i-mutation; "e" drops out before loss of medial "h" can occur)

Like *fōn*, *beran* has 2nd and 3rd person forms that change stem vowel in the present due to i-mutation: *bir(e)st* and *bir(e)ð*. Like *healdan*, *secgan*, "to say," has twin forms for the 2nd and 3rd person present: *sægst / segst* and *sægeð / segð*.

In general, variants from the stem of the infinitive in the formation of the 2nd and 3rd person present tense are due to either i-mutation (vowels) or gemination (consonants). Thus the 2nd and 3rd person present tense forms are among the trickiest to learn in Old English; luckily, you are well on your way to mastering them.

Grimm's Law

In the first half of the 19ᵗʰ century, Jakob and Wilhelm Grimm set upon two major tasks that would come to define (and in many senses create) German literature and linguistics as a national project. While they first became famous for their collections of *Märchen*, or German folk-tales, the university-professor brothers also set out to study the shared roots underlying all branches of the family tree of the Germanic languages. As expert linguists and historians of language, they created the first systematic German dictionary, the *Deutsches Wö rterbuch*, which gave etymologies and showed the development of German words through various sound and spelling shifts.

In his studies, Jakob Grimm came to recognize a consistency in the distribution of consonants that set apart the Germanic family tree from other Indo-European languages such as Latin. Where non-Germanic languages used certain letters, the Germanic languages consistently featured a different set of letters that revealed near uniform changes in sound; Jakob Grimm was able to categorize and explain this linguistic shift.

We will simplify the statement of Grimm's Law into basic differences from a few familiar Latin nouns:

d → *t*	dentem → *tōþ*	[tooth]
g → *c*	genus → *cnēow*	[generation; knee]
p → *f*	piscis → *fisc*	[fish]
t → *Ð / þ*	frater → *brōÐor*	[brother]
gh → *g* [velar]	hostis → *gæst*	[stranger; enemy / guest]

(**Note**: the above is not a complete list of Grimm's Law changes.) Although the shift into the Germanic lang-uages was uniform, further development in consonants took place that created discrepancies between German and Old English forms, such as found in 'Vater' and *fæder*-where we might have expected *fæÐer* in analogy to *brōÐor*.

Verner's Law

Working from Grimm's Law, the Danish philologer Karl Verner was able to explain these "exceptions" to the rule. Verner's Law relies on the difference between **voiced** and **voiceless** consonants and on the placement of **stress** (emphasis of one syllable over another in a word). Let us study two pairs of Modern English words involving "s" and "x" to see how stress changes sound:

| díssolute | [s] | dissólve | [z] |
| éxercise | [ks] | exért | [gz] |

When the consonant in question comes after the stress, it is **voiceless** as in "dissolute" and "exercise"; when the consonant comes before the stress, the consonant is **voiced** as in "dissolve" and "exert."

In proto-Old English, the consonants *h, s,* and *ð* can be affected by these shifts in stress and voicing which create the 'exceptions' to Grimm's Law. We can see the results of these shifts most clearly in the principal parts of the **strong verbs** *wrēon*, "to reveal," *cēosan*, "to choose," and *sniðan*, "to cut":

	infinitive	pret 3 sg.	pret 3 pl.	past part.
h → g	*wrēon*	*wrāh*	*wrigon*	*wrigen*
s → r	*cēosan*	*cēas*	*curon*	*coren*
ð → d	*snīðan*	*snāð*	*snidon*	*sniden*

Verner saw the connection between the location of the *Germanic stress, originally on the 2nd syllable in the third and fourth principle parts, and the irregularity of the consonants in the medial position. He hypothesized that a shift in stress to the 1st syllable only came *after* the consonant change from voiceless *h*, *s*, and *ð* to voiced *g*, *r*, and *d* had taken place in the proto-Old English words. Thus, the Old English forms still display the shift to Verner's Law even as the stress is now put on the 1st syllable.

Nonetheless, adding to our confusion, the Modern English forms have frequently moved back to the Grimm's Law letters by a process of **levelling** which removes anomalies. A good example is *frēosan*, which has taken its Verner's Law form for the pret. 3 pl. *fruron* back to "frozen" in Modern English, thereby maintaining a voiced medial consonant even as it reverts to the voiced "s" form that is "z." Similarly affected is *lēosan*, "to lose", and its past participle *loren*. This is why we have the odd pair "lost and 'forlorn;"; the latter did not undergo levelling as it belonged to the weak verb *forlorian*.

Let's take a final look at the nouns "brother" and "father" and see why they are different in Old English:

Latin	frāter	*Gmc	brūder	OE	brōðor	MnE	brother
Latin	*patér*	*Gmc*	*vater*	*OE*	*fæder*	*MnE*	*father*

In Latin, the stress falls on the long ā of the first syllable in "frāter" but on the 2nd syllable of the short **e** of "pater." Thus, as the **t** in "frāter" develops regularly into the **ð** in "brōðor" by Grimm's Law, the same process occurs in "pater" as the **t** develops into **ð** in proto-Old English **fæðer*, with the corollary that becuase the **ð** comes before the stress on the 2nd syllable, the consonant becomes voiced **d** in keeping with Verner's Law. As above, Grimm's Law explains the change from **p** in "pater" to **f** in *fæder* and the voiced variant of **f** that is **v** in "vater"; similarly, the **b** in *Gmc "brūder" is simply a voiced variant of the **f**' in "frater."

Old English to Middle English to Modern English

The sound changes we discuss above help explain how primitive Germanic evolved into Old English. A detailed description of how Old English then evolved into Middle English and Middle English into Modern English could be a book in itself. But, greatly simplified, there are two events that mark the major changes: the **Norman Conquest** of 1066 and the **Great Vowel Shift** of 1400-1600.

As we noted in Chapter 1, in 1066 William the Conqueror invaded England and made Norman French the language of the aristocracy and the law courts. But Old English was never really given up for French, and the two languages co-existed (with only a minority of bilingual speakers). Over the next century and a half, Old English changed significantly: **inflections** started to wear down and word order consequently grew in importance; a massive Latinate vocabulary became Anglicized, especially for technical matters such as administration, architecture and chivalry; last, as French vowel pronunciation started to win out, spelling rules, or **orthography**, loosened considerably.

We now term the resulting blended language Middle English, though it was really a superstructure of French vocabulary and pronunciation set on the groundwork of an Old English that had changed substantially as a result of interference from the Old Norse spoken by Danish colonists in the ninth through eleventh centuries. This is why all the most commonly used words such as pronouns, articles and prepositions in Modern English are virtually unchanged from Old English even as the sheer number of words available to Middle English grew enormously. Middle English also retained and amplified dialectical variations, with the South, including London, taking up French forms and pronunciation enthusiastically, and with the North holding on to its Germanic and Viking heritage.

Then, in the years between 1400 and 1600, Middle English underwent a major change in the pronunciation of vowels. The high vowels **i** and **u** became diphthongs (**aj** and **aw**) and the long vowels moved up towards the positions in the mouth where the previous high vowels had been. In addition, the back vowel **a** moved to the front of the mouth.

The **Great Vowel Shift** did not affect every word in the language: some words had already undergone a process called Early Middle English Vowel Shortening, which blocked the effects of the Great Vowel Shift (which is why we say "crime" with a long vowel, but "criminal" with a short vowel: "criminal" had been previously shortened). But the Great Vowel Shift can be credited for most of the differences between Chaucer's English and Shakespeare's. The differences between Shakespeare's English and our own are not as striking as those between Old and Middle or Middle and Modern English, but they do exist and were influenced by regular processes of sound change like those we have just discussed.

ANSWERS TO EXERCISES

Chapter 4: Some exercises to practice recognizing the parts of speech

Label each part of speech in the sentences below.

Parts of speech: **noun, pronoun, verb, adjective, adverb, preposition, conjunction**. Mark articles as demonstrative pronouns.

1. Prn N   V   Prn Adj   N   Prep Prn Adj   N
The king ruled the great kingdom for a long time.

2. Prn   N   V   V   Prep Prn N*   N
The battle was fought at   the thorn tree.
[* "Thorn tree" is a **compound noun**. "Thorn" is fulfilling an adjectival role (modifying "tree") but is in this case a noun. "Thorny" would be the correct adjectival form.]

3.   N   V   Prep   P   Adj   N
    Alfred struggled against the rapacious Vikings.

4. Adj   N   V   Prep Prn Adj   N
    Many monks traveled   to   the ruined city.

5.   Adj*   N   V   Adj   Prep   Prn Adj   N
    Alfred's warriors fought fiercely against the evil invaders.
    [* "Alfred's" is in fact a noun in the **genitive** case but here it is
    fulfilling the role of an adjective, describing "warriors."]

6. Prn N   V   N*   Conj   N   Prep   Prn   N
    The king spread learning and culture through the land.
    [* "Learning" is a **gerund**, a verb being used as a noun.]

7. Adj   N   V   N   V Prn Prn
    Some historians say   Alfred is the first

    Adj   N   Prep   N
    true   king   of   England.

8. Prep   N   Conj Adj   N   N   V
    With   effort   and   hard work, Alfred learned

    V*   Adj   Adj   N
    to read difficult Latin books.
    [* In this sentence "to" is not a preposition but part of the
    infinitive form of the verb "to read."]

9.   Adj*   N   V   Prn Adj   N   Prep
    Alfred's father   made   the long journey   to

    N   Conj   V   Adj
    Rome   and   returned quickly.
    [* "Alfred's" is a noun in the **genitive** case, here fulfilling the role
    of an adjective (see above, sentence 5).]

10. Prn Adj*   N   V   V   V   V   Prep   N
    The Alfred jewel may have been created   for   Alfred.
    [* "Alfred" here is a noun being used as an adjective to modify
    "jewel".]

Chapter 5: Some exercises to practice recognizing word functions.

Label the subjects, verbs and direct objects in the sentences below.

1.   S   **V**   *V*
    <u>Alfred</u> **killed** *the Viking.*

2.   <u>S</u>   **V**   *DO*
    <u>The ruler of the West Saxons</u> **sent** *a message.*

3.   *S*   **V**   *OP*
    Guthorm **attacked** *the English king.*

4.   <u>S</u>   **V**   *DO*   **V**
    <u>The herald</u> **struck** *his shield* and **spoke.**

5.   <u>S</u>   **V**   *DO*
    <u>The warriors</u> **dropped** *their swords.*

Label the subjects, verbs, direct objects and indirect objects / objects of prepositions in the following sentences.

1.   <u>S</u>   **V**   *V*   ***OP***
    <u>Alfred</u> **killed** *the Viking* with ***his sword.***

2.   <u>S</u>   **V**   *DO*   **IO**
    <u>The ruler of the West Saxons</u> **sent** a *message* to ***Guthorm.***

3.   *S*   **V**   ***OP***   ***OP***
    Guthorm **negotiated** with ***the English king*** about ***the treaty.***

4.   <u>S</u>   **V**   *DO*   **V**   *DO*
    <u>The herald</u> **struck** *his shield* and **inspired** *the warriors.*

5.   <u>S</u>   **V**   *DO*   ***OP***
    <u>The warriors</u> **dropped** *their swords* on ***the ground.***

Label the subjects, verbs, direct objects, indirect objects / objects of prepositions, and modifiers in the following sentences.

1. S   **V**   *M*   *M*   *DO*   **M** **M** *OP*
    <u>Alfred</u> **killed** *the vicious Viking* with **his old** *sword*.

2. *M*   *M*   <u>S</u>   **V** *M* *DO*   **M**   *IO*
    <u>The</u> <u>kind</u> <u>ruler</u> **sent** *a message* to **brave** **Guthorm**.

3. *M*   <u>S</u>   **V**   **M**   *M*
    <u>Wise</u> <u>Guthorm</u> **negotiated** with **the** *trustworthy*

    M   *OP*   *M*   *M*   *OP*
    English *king* *the* *important* *treaty*.

4. *M*   *M*   <u>S</u>   **V** *M* *M* *DO*   **M**
    <u>The</u> <u>grizzled</u> <u>herald</u> **struck** *his linden shield* and **loudly**

    V   *M*   *M*   *DO*
    inspired *the* *tired* *warriors*.

5. *M*   *M*   <u>S</u>   **M**   **V** *M*   *M*   *DO*
    <u>The</u> <u>hungry</u> <u>warriors</u> **quickly** **dropped** *their notched swords*

    M   *M*   *OP*
    onto *the* *wet* *ground*.

Chapter 6: Some exercises to practice using endings to determine the sense of a sentence.

"Translate" the sentences below into correct Modern English word order.

1. <u>Vikings (direct object)</u> <u>Alfred (subject)</u> fought against
    Alfred fought against the Vikings.

2. gave <u>to the king (indirect object)</u> <u>the monks (subject)</u> <u>the jewel (direct object)</u>
   The monks gave the jewel to the king.

3. <u>Wulfgar (subject)</u> <u>to Alfred (indirect object)</u> pledged <u>his support (direct object)</u>
   Wulfgar pledged his support to Alfred

4. <u>English warriors (subject)</u> <u>many Viking ships (direct object)</u> burned
   English warriors burned many Viking ships.

5. ate <u>crows (subject)</u> <u>many bodies (direct object)</u>
   Crows ate many bodies.

Chapter 6: Some exercises for identifying cases.

Label each word in the sentences below with its appropriate case: **nominative**, **genitive**, **dative** or **instrumental**. Remember that verbs, adverbs and prepositions do not need to be identified with a case.

1. N   N   A   A
   Few kings rule large kingdoms well.

2. N   N   N   A
   One great king ruled England.

3. N   N   G   A
   Skilled smiths made Alfred's sword.

4. N   N   A   A   I   I   I
   The warrior struck the Viking with the heavy axe.

5. N   A   A   D   D
   Alfred gave the jewel to the bishop.

6.   N   N   D   N

   Before the king arrived in Athelney, he

          A   A

   had   many   adventures.

7. N   N   N   A

   Many fierce Vikings invaded England

          D   D   D

   after the eighth century.

8. N   N   N   N

   Some brave warriors and desperate

    N   A   A

   families   fought   the   invaders.

9. N   N   G   G

   The   swords   of the   Vikings   were stained with

     D   D   G   G

   the   blood   of   the   monks.

10.   N   A   A   G

   Scholars worked hard to rebuild the culture of England.

Chapter 7 Translation Practice

1. Slǣpþ hē nǣfre.
   He never sleeps.
   [Remember that word order is more flexible in Old English than in Modern English.]

2. Sum mann fēoll on īse.
   A certain man fell on ice.
   ["īse" is dative because it is a location. The man slipped while on the ice; he didn't fall on to it, or "īse" would be in the accusative case - contrast with sentence 5 below.]

3. Ðā hīe ðider cōmon.
   Then they came thither (to that place).

4. Sē kyng geaf gryþ Olāfe.
   The king gave quarter (mercy) to Olaf.

5. And hē āstah on heofonas.
   And he rose into the heavens.
   ["on heofonas" is accusative because the subject is moving -
   contrast to sentence 2 above.]

6. Hē eft gebēte.
   He repented afterwards.

Chapter 9 Translation Practice

1. Ðā ēodon hīe ūt.
   Then they went out.

2. Hwær sindon seledrēamas?
   Where are hall-joys?

3. Hē on þā duru ēode.
   He went in through the door.

4. Hiera mǣgas him mid wǣron.
   Their kinsmen were with him/them.
   [From this sentence alone you cannot tell whether the object
   is singular or plural.]

5. Hē wrǣcca wæs.
   He was an exile.

6. Hīe þā swā dydon.
   They did just so.

7. Yfel dēþ sē unwrītere.
   The bad scribe does harm.

8. Gā on þā ceastre.
   Go then into that castle/fortified town/walled place.
   [Note that the verb is in the imperative mood. Just as in Modern English, the subject (you) is missing.]

9. Hiera ryhtfæderencyn gǣþ tō Cerdice.
   Their ancestry goes (back) to Cerdic.

10. Hwī dēst þū swā?
    Why are you doing so?
    [A more literal, but archaic, translation is "Why doest thou so?"]

Chapter 10 Translation Practice

1. Sēo ylce rōd siþþan, þe Ōswold þǣr ārǣrde, on wurþmynte þǣr stōd.
   Afterwards the same cross, which Oswald raised there, stood there in reverence.
   [It often helps to move adverbs of time to the beginning of the sentence; sēo can refer to the grammatical gender of the noun.]

2. Gesēoh þū, cyning, hwelc þēos lār sie þe ūs nū bodad is.
   See you, king, of what sort this lore, which is now proclaimed to us, may be.
   [Your first approximation for the translation of the sentence might be: "See you, king, of what sort this lore may be which is now proclaimed to us." Then rearrange into Modern English word order.]

3. Wæs hē, sē mon, in weoruldhāde geseted oþ þā tīde þe hē
   wæs gelȳfdre ylde.
   He, the man, was located in secular life, until the time in
   which he was of advanced old age.

4. Đonne cymeþ Ifling of þǣm mere þe Trūso standeþ in staþe.
   Then comes the Ifling River from that lake by which Truso
   stands on the shore.

5. Ic wolde helpan þæs þe þǣr unscyldig wǣre, ond ne herian
   þone þe hine yflode.
   I wished to help whomever was not guilty and not to praise
   the one who did evil to him.
   [The object of *helpan* often takes the genitive case, here *þæs*,
   'to give help to the one who';
   the verb *wǣre* is in the subjunctive because the sense is
   open-ended, ie. referring to 'whomever.']

6. And þā þe gesāwene synt ofer þæt gōde land, ðā synd ðe
   þæt word gehȳraþ.
   And those who are seen (visible) over that good land, those
   are those ones who hear the word.

7. And hē cwæþ, 'Gehȳre, sē þe ēaran hæbbe tō gehȳranne.'
   And he said, "Hear! He who has ears for hearing."
   [*tō gehȳranne* is an example of the inflected infinitive.]

8. Þā hē þā þās andswere onfēng, ðā ongan hē sōna singan, in
   herenesse Godes Scyppendes.
   When he received that answer, then he began immediately
   to sing in praise of God, of the Creator.

9. Hē þæt wel þafode, and hēo hine in þæt mynster onfēng mid his gōdum.

   He well agreed to that, and she received him in that monastery with his goods.

   ["In" + accuastive case means 'motion toward' or "into".]

10. On þȳs gēare-þæt wæs ymb twelf mōnað þæs þe hīe on þǣm, ēastrīce geweorc geworht hæfdon-Norþhymbre ond Ēastengle hæfdon Ælfrede cyninge āþas geseald.

    In this year - that was twelve months after which they had made a defensive work in the east kingdom-Northumbria and East Anglia had given oaths to King Alfred.

    ["Ēastrīce" is a **locative dative**, that is, it refers to a stationary (non-moving) thing: they made (+ accusative) a fortification, in (+ dative) the east kingdom. Note that the word 'in' is implicit in this phrase; it need not be spelled out since the locative dative already includes its presence.]

Chapter 12 Translation Practice: Answers

1. And wearþ sē cyng swȳþe gram wiþ þā burhware.
   And the king became very angry against the citizenry.

2. Hē wæs swȳþe spēdig man.
   He was a very prosperous man.

3. Ac hē is snel and swift and swīþe lēoht.
   But he is quick and swift and very light.

4. Ðā wurdon þā mynstermen micclum āfyrhte.
   Then the monks became greatly frightened.

5. Ond þǣr wearþ Hēahmund bisceop ofslægen ond fela gōdra monna.
   And there Bishop Heahmund was slain and many good men.

[A literal translation of *wearþ ofslægen* would be "became slain." *Fela gōdra monna* is an example of a **partitive genitive,** discussed below in Chapter 19. In this case, translate as a simple plural.]

6. And þæt bȳne land is ēasteweard brādost.
   And that cultivated land is broadest in the east.

7. Hē wæs mid þǣm fyrstum mannum on þǣm lande.
   He was with the first men in that land.
   [*mid* + dative case *þǣm* could be translated as "among those"]

8. Sē hwæl biþ micle lǣssa þonne ōþre hwalas.
   The whale is much smaller than other whales.

9. Đā bēoþ swȳþe dȳre mid Finnum, for þǣm hȳ fōþ þā wildan hrānas mid.
   Those are very precious to the Finns/Saami because with them they catch those wild reindeer.
   [A literal translation of *mid Finnum* would be "with the Finns," "to the Finns" is given to make the translation idiomatic in Modern English, where "precious" takes the preposition "to."]

10. Wæs þǣr in nēaweste untrumra monna hūs.
    In the vicinity there was a house of unwell men.
    [The subject is the last word in the sentence because *hūs* is the only noun in the nominative case.]

Chapter 13 Translation Practice

1. Ne dohte hit nū lange ac wæs here and hunger, bryne and blōdgyte.
   Now it did not avail for long, but there was war and hunger, fire and bloodshed.

2. Hīo hæfde þǣr swīþe micle werod hire þegna and ēac
   ōþerra mædena.
   She had there a very great company of her thanes and also
   of other maidens.

3. Hē gӯmþ grǣdlīce his tēolunge, his gafoles, his gebytla; hē
   berӯpþ ðā wanspēdigan.
   He cares greedily for his tillage, his tribute, his buildings; he
   plunders those poor ones.

4. Fela gedreccednyssa and earfoþnyssa becumaþ on þissere
   worulde.
   Many tribulations and hardships befall in this world.

5. Ūre ieldran, ðā ðe ðās stōwe ǣr hīoldon, hīe lofodon
   wīsdōm.
   Our ancestors, those who previously held this place, they
   loved wisdom.

Chapter 14 Translation Practice

1. Ðǣre sunnan beorhtnys, mōnan lēoht, and ealra tungla sind
   gemǣne þām rīcan and þām hēanan.
   The sun's brightness, the light of the moon, and of all the
   stars are common to the rich and the poor.

2. Ne is þǣr on þām londe lāþgenīþla, ne wōp ne wracu.
   Nor is there in that lands a single foe (partitive genitive: one
   of foes), nor weeping nor suffering.

3. Lētan him behindan hrāw bryttigean salowigpādan, ðone
   sweartan hræfn, hyrnednebban, and ðone hasupādan earn.
   They left behind them corpses to share among the
   darkfeathered one, the black raven, horn-beaked, and the
   grey-coated eagle.

[A literal translation would be "left by them behind." The Anglo-Saxon writer uses this construction because he wants to emphasize the corpses, not the ones doing the leaving.]

4. Faraþ ardlice, and befrīnað be ðam cilde, and þonne gē hit gemētað, cȳðað mē, þæt ic mæge mē tō him gebiddan.
    Go quickly and ask about that child, and when you find it, inform me, so that I may pray to him.

5. Ðā geworden wæs þæt hīe hine eft betȳndon on þām carcerne.
    Then it so happened that they afterwards imprisoned him in that jail.

Chapter 15 Translation Practice

1. Ðȳ ilcan sumera forwearþ nō læs þonne xx scipa mid monnum mid ealle be þām sūþriman.
    That same summer perished no less than 20 ships with men and with all along that south-coast.
    [*mid ealle* could be taken as "with all goods."]

2. Hē meahte hearpian þæt sē wudu wagode, ond ðā stānas hīe styredon for þȳ swēge.
    He was able to harp so that the forest shook, and the stones themselves stirred because of that sound.
    [The phrase *ða stanas hie* is literally "the stones, they." It is a reflexive construction, and is thus translated as "the stones themselves."]

3. Byrnan hringdon, gūþsearo gumena; gāras stōdon; sǣmanna searo, samod ætgædere.
    Byrnies rang, the wargear of men; spears stood; war-gear of the sea-men, altogether.

4. Þā ongan sēo abbudysse clyppan and lufian þā Godes gyfe in þæm menn.
   Then the abbess began to embrace and love that gift of God in that man.

5. Ond hē lȳtle werede unīeþelīce æfter wudum fōr ond on mōrfæstenum.
   And with a little troop he fared with difficulty into the woods and into the marsh-fastness.

Chapter 16 Translation Practice

1. On þæm mōrum eardiaþ Finnas.
   Finns dwell on those moors.

2. Ðā wendon forþ wlance þegenas; unearge men efston georne.
   Then proud thanes went forth; brave men hastened eagerly.

3. Onscuna þū ā lēasunga.
   Always keep yourself from lying.
   [Because the sentence is in the imperative mood, which implies one "you" in the sentence, the þū that appears is interpreted as a reflexive: "yourself."]

4. On þȳs gēare, Norþhymbre ond Ēastengle hæfdon Ælfrede cyninge āþas geseald.
   In this year, Northumbrians and East-Angles had given oaths to King Alfred.

5. Ne recce ic hwæt hī dēmen.
   Nor might I care what they might judge (deem).
   [The two subjunctives (recce and demen) give the two "mights" in the translation.]

6. Paulīnus sē biscop Godes word bodade ond lǣrde ond sē cyning elde þā gȳt tō gelȳfanne.

   Paulinus the bishop proclaimed and taught God's word and yet the king still hesitated then in believing.

7. Nū gif þū ǣnig ðincg hǣfst of ðæs hālgan reliquium, syle mē.

   Now if you have any piece of that holy relic, give them to me.

   ["Reliquium" is Latin, not Old English.]

8. And hē his cyricean getimbrade sēo on āre Scæ Andree þæs apostoles gehālgad is.

   And he built his church which is consecrated in honor of St. Andrew the apostle.

   ["Sēo" is feminine because it agrees in *grammatical* gender with "cyricean." "Is" plus the past participle "getimbrade" creates a **perfect** tense, an action that has been completed.]

9. And hē nele swā micclum swā wē geearniaþ ūs geyrsian.

   And he does not want to be as greatly angry at us as we are deserving.

10. Hē cwæð þæt hē būde on þǣm lande norþweardum wiþ þā Westsǣ.

    He said that he dwelled in that land northwards by the West Sea.

Chapter 17 Translation Practice

1. Til bið sē ðe his trēowe gehealdeð.
   Good is he who holds his pledge.

2. Hē fōr tō Rōme and ðǣr gesæt, ond his līc līð on Sancta Marīan circean.
   He went to Rome and there stayed, and his body lies in St. Mary's church.

3. Wearð ðā fordrifen on an īglond ūt on ðǣre Wendelsǣ.
   Those became swept away on an island out in the Wendel Sea.

4. And ðonne hē his byrnsweord getȳð and ðās world ealle ðurh-slȳhð.
   And then he drew his flaming sword and smote through all the world.

5. Hī ðā somod ealle ongunnon cohhetan, cirman hlūde ond gristbitian.
   Then they together all began to shout, to cry out loudly and gnash teeth.

6. Gē ealdras tonymað ðā gatu, and ūp āhebbað ðā ēcan gatu.
   You princes open those gates, and lift up those eternal gates.

7. For ðōn ðū ūs ðus dydest, wē hit ðē forgyldað.
   Because as you did thus for us, we will repay it to you.
   [There is no future tense in Old English, but the sense of the sentence allows us to interpret the present tense as the future.]

8. Nū gē ðus feor hider on ūrne eard in becōmon.
   Now you have come thus far hither into our land.

9. Þā hēt hēo gesomnian ealle þā gelǣrdestan menn and þa leorneras, and him andweardum hēt secgan þæt swefn.
   Then she commanded those most learned men and those students all together, and commanded them to answer about that dream.

10. Þā sē wyrm onwōc, wrōht wæs genīwad.
   Then the dragon awoke, strife was renewed.

Chapter 18 Translation Practice

1. Hwæt sceal ic singan?
    What shall I sing?

2. Þā on morgenne gehīerdun þæt þæs cyninges þegnas, þe
    him beæftan wærun, þæt sē cyning ofslægen wæs.
    Then in the morning the kings' thanes, those who were left
    behind him, heard that the king had been slain.

3. Ond hīe būtū geflīemdon ond longe on dæg sige āhton.
    And they put both [armies] to flight and on that day had
    victory.

4. And ūs is mycel nēdþearf þæt wē ūs sylfe geðencean and
    gemunan.
    And it is greatly needful for us that we think and remember
    about ourselves.

5. Þā cirdon hīe ūp on ðā ēa, for þǣm hīe nō dorston forþ bi
    þǣre ēa siglan for unfriþe.
    Then they turned up into that river, because they did not
    dare to sail forth from the river due to hostility.

GLOSSARY OF GRAMMAR TERMS

accusative

The direct object case, the accusative case is used to indicate direct receivers of an action. The accusative case also indicates "motion towards," can be the object of the preposition "to" and can indicate the passage of time.

adjective

An adjective is a word used to describe a noun. "Royal," "golden," "lofty," "powerful," "hardy" and "strong" are all adjectives.

adverb

An adverb is a word used to describe a verb or adjective. "Slowly," "steadily," "angrily," "powerfully" and "very" are all adverbs. Words that indicate time, such as "then," "when," "later," and "before" are also adverbs.

analytic language

A language in which grammatical relationships are indicated by word order (i.e., "the dog ate the cat" means something different from "the cat ate the dog") is an analytic language.

article

A word linked with a noun or nouns used to identify a word as a noun and also indicate whether that noun is definite or indefinite. Modern English has a definite article ("the") and an indefinite article ("a" / "an"). In this grammar book we classify Old English articles as demonstrative pronouns because in Old English an article can stand on its own without a noun.

auxiliary verb

These verbs, sometimes known as helping verbs, are combined with the main verb in a sentence. Auxiliary verbs often give information about time, completion of an action or probability of an action. In the sentence "Alfred had ruled for ten years," "had" is the auxiliary verb.

back vowel

A vowel pronounced in the back of the mouth. In Old English *a, 0,* and *u* are back vowels.

case agreement

If a noun is in one case, the pronouns and adjectives grammatically related to that noun will also be in that case. For example, if a noun is in the genitive case, a demonstrative or adjective describing that noun would also be in the genitive case.

case

The endings on a noun, pronouns or adjective indicate which case it belongs to. In turn, the case indicates what function the word is performing in the sentence, whether it is the subject (nominative), the direct object (accusative), the indirect object or object of a preposition (dative), or if it is a possessive (genitive) form.

clause

A clause is a dependent part of a sentence that has its own subject and predicate but still depends on the main part of the sentence. (A predicate can be simply a verb, or it can include a verb and an object.)

conjugating

Verbs change form depending upon who performs an action (the person of the verb), how many perform the action (the number of the verb), whether the action was in the past or the present (the tense of the verb), and whether the verb is a statement, command, or prediction (the mood of the verb). Writing out the various forms of a verb for each of its possible grammatical uses is called conjugating the verb.

conjunction

A conjunction is a connecting word: "and," "but," "or," and "nor" are all conjunctions.

consonant

Sounds in a language can be classified as vowels, semi-vowels (also called "liquids") or consonants. Consonants are characterized by the occlusion, obstruction or diversion of the flow of air from the lungs through the mouth and nose.

dative

The indirect object and prepositional case, the dative case is used to indicate indirect receivers of action and objects of prepositions. The dative is also used to indicate the location of non-moving objects (locative dative).

declension

A list of all the possible case endings for a noun, adjective or pronoun is called a declension.

determiner

The definite and indefinite articles ("the" and "a") are also called determiners.

demonstrative

A pronoun that 'points to' another word or indicates relationships of proximity is a demonstrative. "This," "that," "these" and "those" are demonstratives. In this grammar book we treat articles (Modern English "the," "a," "an"; Old English *sē*, *þæt* and *sēo*) as demonstrative pronouns.

digraph

Two letters used to represent one sound are called a digraph. "Th" and "ch" in Modern English are digraphs.

direct object

The direct object is the receiver of the action. In the sentence "Alfred ate the cakes," "cakes" is the direct object."

dual

One of the three possible numbers for an Old English pronoun (the others are singular and plural). The dual form is used to indicate two closely associated persons-two people working or fighting together, husband and wife, or lovers.

ending

Also called suffixes, endings or inflections are groups of letters attached to the ends of words to indicate the grammatical relationships.

facsimile

A photographic reproduction of a manuscript is called a facsimile.

feminine

A grammatical gender category. Feminine words can (in the case of pronouns) indicate the actual gender of a pronoun (ie. we use "she" to indicate a female agent), but they also can simply indicate the grammatical category into which a word fits.

front vowel

A vowel pronounced in the front of the mouth. In Old English *e* and *i* are back vowels.

function word

What we are calling "function words" are prepositions and conjunctions that don't mean anything in themselves but serve to indicate the ways other words relate to each other. Prepositions indicate relationships, and conjunctions join things together. In the sentences "Alfred fought with the Vikings and won the battle by the thorn tree," "with" and "by" are prepositions that indicate relationships (where the battle was fought and whom it was fought against) and "and" indicates that two parts of the sentence are joined together.

genitive

The possession case, the genitive case is used to indicate ownership. Some verbs also take genitive (rather than accusative) objects.

gerund

A verb used as a noun (in Modern English with an "-ing" ending) is a gerund. In the sentence "Reading was Alfred's favorite leisure activity," "reading" is a gerund.

gloss

Translations, interpretations or descriptions written above a line of text are called glosses.

helping verb

These verbs, sometimes known as auxiliary verbs, are combined with the main verb in a sentence. Helping verbs often give information about time, completion of an action or probability of an action. In the sentence "Alfred had ruled for ten years," "had" is the helping verb.

if-clause

One of the ways Modern English handles the subjunctive mood is via the "if-clause," which indicates possibility or conditionality rather than certainty.

imperative

The imperative mood is used for commands: "Walk to the store!" is in the imperative mood. In both Modern English and Old English the second-person subject of the sentence ("you") can be deleted in sentences in the imperative mood.

indicative

The indicative mood is used for statements: "I walk quickly" is in the indicative mood.

indirect object

The indirect object is the secondary receiver of the action. In the sentence "Alfred carried the sword to the battle," "battle" is the indirect object (and "sword," which is receiving the action, is the direct object). Indirect objects are often called "objects of prepositions" because in Modern English we use prepositions to indicate the sort of action being secondarily received: in the phrases "to the battle," "with the sword," "under the thorn tree," "by the river," "battle," "sword," "tree," and "river" are the objects of their respective prepositions.

infinitive

These verbs indicate action that can happen at any point in time (hence, "infinitive"). In Modern English they are constructed by adding the word "to" to the root form of the verb. In Old English the infinitive will end in -*an* or -*ian*.

inflected infinitive

Some grammar books call this the "Old English Gerund," which is not precisely correct, but gives the idea of what the inflected infinitive is communicating. Regularly preceded by the preposition "to," the inflected infinitive is a verb form generally used to express the idea of purpose.

inflected language

Instead of relying on word order to indicate relationships (as do analytic languages) inflected languages attach endings (inflections) to words to indicate grammatical relationships.

instrumental

The instrumental case (which, in Old English, usually takes the same inflections as the dative case), is used to indicate things that are being used ("instruments").

interrogative pronoun

A pronoun that takes the place of a personal pronoun to indicate a question. For example, "who" takes the place of "he" or "she," changing statements like "He killed the Vikings" or "She fought that battle" into the questions "Who killed the Vikings?" and "Who found the battle?"

intervocalic

A consonant that occurs between two vowels is called "intervocalic." In Old English, intervocalic "f" is pronounced like Modern English "v".

linking verb

These verbs ("is," "was," "are" and other forms of the verb "to be") are used to rename or describe a subject; one useful way to analyze them is to think of linking verbs as being the same as an equals sign (=) between two things.

liquid

Also called a "semi-vowel," a liquid falls between a vowel and a consonant: the air flow from the lungs and through the mouth or nose is only partially obstructed, unlike a consonant, in which the stream is obstructed, or a vowel, in which it is not obstructed. Liquids in Modern English and Old English include "r," "l" and "w."

long vowel

A long vowel is one in which the duration of its pronunciation is relatively longer than that of a short vowel.

macron

A horizontal bar over the top of a vowel to indicate a long vowel (ā, ǣ, ē, ī, ō, ū) is called a macron. Macrons to indicate vowel length are not found in Anglo-Saxon manuscripts.

main verb

These verbs express the main action of a sentence or clause

manuscript

A hand-written document is called a manuscript. Anglo-Saxon manuscripts were written on parchment (sheep skin) or vellum (calf skin).

masculine

A grammatical gender category. Masculine words can (in the case of pronouns) indicate the actual gender of a pronoun (i.e., we use "he" to indicate a male subject), but they also can simply indicate the grammatical category into which a word fits.

minor noun

Nouns that do not fall into the major declensions (strong and weak) are considered "minor declension" nouns.

modal verb

These verbs (also known as modal auxiliaries) can be used to indicate additional information about the verb such as probability or the completeness of an action. "Should," "would," "could," "may" and "might" are all modals in Modern English.

modifier

Modifiers describe subjects, verbs and objects. In the sentence "With his old sword, Alfred quickly killed the Viking," "old" is an adjective that modifies "sword" (it describes the condition of the sword), and "quickly" is an adverb that modifies "killed" (it explains how the killing was done). Adjectives describe subjects and objects; adverbs describe verbs and adjectives. In Old English certain pronouns (demonstratives) are used as modifiers: In the sentence "this sword belongs to that man," "this" describes the sword and "that" describes the man. Likewise "a," "an," and "the," which we call articles in Modern English, are, in Old English grammar, special pronouns (demonstratives) that are used as modifiers: "The sword" is different from "a sword" because the modifiers "the" and "a" are providing different descriptions. Genitives are an important sub-set of modifiers in Old English. Genitives are possessives: they indicate ownership. A noun with a genitive ending, like the Modern English *'s*, is used as an adjective to modify another noun. In the sentence "Alfred's sword was old," "Alfred's" is a genitive: a noun (Alfred) has had the genitive ending ('s) added to it. A good rule of thumb for dealing with the genitive is to translate it as "of X" where "X" is the noun that has the genitive ending. Thus "Alfred's sword" could be translated as "the sword of Alfred."

mood

The mood of a verb (indicative, subjunctive, imperative) indicates whether the verb is a fact, wish, possibility or command.

neuter

A grammatical gender category. Neuter words do not follow either the masculine or feminine patterns that indicate the grammatical category into which a word fits.

nominative

The naming case. The nominative case is used for subjects and for predicate nominatives (words that rename the subject of the sentence).

noun

A noun is a naming word. "King," "Alfred," "crown," "kingdom" and "power" are all nouns.

noun phrase

A noun and any associated adjectives and demonstratives make up a noun phrase.

number

The number of the word indicates whether it is singular, plural or dual.

object of preposition

Indirect objects are often called "objects of prepositions" because in Modern English we use prepositions to indicate the sort of action being secondarily received: in the phrases "to the battle," "with the sword," "under the thorn tree," "by the river" "battle," "sword," "tree" and "river" are the objects of their respective prepositions.

Old English gerund

Another name of the inflected infinitive, the Old English Gerund is a verb form usually used to express the idea of purpose.

palatal g

A "g" sound pronounced with the tongue touching the hard palate is called palatal g. Palatal g sounds like the "y" in "yes."

paleograph

y The study of ancient writing is called paleography.

paradigm

A paradigm is a list of all the possible grammatical forms of a word. It is usually arranged in a table, so that you can easily look up the forms that you need to translate.

participle

Verbs used as adjectives are called participles. They can be either past or present. "Alfred's aching back" is an example of a present participle; "Alfred's tired eyes" is an example of a past participle.

parts of speech

Every word in a language can be put into one or more categories that explain how that word is used. These categories are the "parts of speech."

person

The person of a verb indicates who is being spoken of. First person = speaker; second person = person being addressed; third person = third person being spoken about.

personal pronoun

A word that stands in for a noun and can be used to designate the first, second or third person is a personal pronoun (contrasted with a demonstrative pronoun, which points out something).

possessive adjective

When forms of the personal pronouns in the genitive are used to modify other words, for example "his book," "her land," "our meeting," they are possessive adjectives. They are declined following the same paradigms as do other adjectives.

predicate nominative

A noun or pronoun in the predicate of the sentence (that is, after the verb) that renames the subject of the sentence is called a predicate nominative. In the sentence "Alfred was king," "king" is the predicate nominative. Predicate nominatives are also called "subject complements." A predicate nominative will take the same case (the nominative) as the noun it renames.

preposition

A preposition is a short explanatory word that indicates things such as location, direction and possession: "with," "to," "under," "over," "by" and "for" are all prepositions.

preterite

The past tense is called, in some grammar books, the preterite.

principal parts

The four parts of an Anglo-Saxon strong verb that must be known in order to construct the verb's paradigm. They are the infinitive, the 3rd person singular past tense, the past tense for all plurals, and the past participle.

pronoun

A pronoun is a word used in place of a noun. "He," "she," "it," "who," "whom," "that," "which," "we," "they" and "us" are all pronouns. This grammar book groups words like "this," "that," "these" and "those," as well as "a," "an" and "the" with the pronouns and calls these words demonstrative pronouns, although grammarians would probably call some of them articles, and linguists would identify them as determiners.

r-declension

The r-declension is one of the minor noun declensions; it includes the "family words" such as "mother" and "father."

radical-consonant

Radical consonant declension nouns are nouns where vowels change in the noun stem (the way that Modern English "foot" changes to "feet" in the plural) either in addition to, or in place of, adding an ending to the stem.

relative clause

A relative clause is a clause that modifies a noun or a pronoun elsewhere in the sentence.

relative pronoun

A relative pronoun is the subject of a relative clause.

rune

A letter in a Germanic / Scandinavian alphabet. Runes were angular, rather than rounded, because they were designed to be cut or scratch onto surfaces.

semi-vowel

Also called a "liquid," a semi-vowel falls between a vowel and a consonant: the air flow from the lungs and through the mouth or nose is only partially obstructed, unlike a consonant, in which the stream is obstructed, or a vowel, in which it is not obstructed. Semi-vowels in Modern English and Old English include "r," "l" and "w."

short vowel

A short vowel is one in which the duration of its pronunciation is relatively shorter than that of a long vowel. A short vowel will not be represented with a macron.

stem

The stem of a word includes only those elements of the word that are unchanged regardless of the word's grammatical function. It is the part of the word onto which endings are attached. The stem is also often called the "root" of the word.

strong adjective

An adjective that is not preceded by a demonstrative is called a strong adjective.

strong noun

Nouns that end with a consonant are usually considered to be strong nouns; they follow the strong noun (masculine, feminine, neuter; or first, second and third) declensions.

strong verb

Verbs in which the stem vowel is changed to indicate different tenses are considered strong verbs.

subject complement

A noun or pronoun in the predicate of the sentence (that is, after the verb) that renames the subject of the sentence is called a subject complement. In the sentence "Alfred was king," "king" is the subject complement. Subject complements are also called "predicate nominatives." A subject complement will be the same case (the nominative) as the noun it renames.

subject

The subject is the "doer" or "actor" in a sentence. In the sentence "Alfred ate the cakes," Alfred is the subject, so it takes the nominative case Nouns and pronouns are used for subjects.

subjunctive

The mood of the verb that indicates possibility, conditionality or probability is called the subjunctive. In Old English it is characterized by the appearance of *e* or *en* in the suffix.

syntax

The rules by which we arrange words to convey meaning are called syntax.

tense

The tense of a verb indicates whether an action occurrs in the past, present or future.

u- declension

The *u*-declension is one of the minor noun declensions. Most *u*-declension nouns end in *u*, although the *u*-declension does contain some other nouns that end in consonants but nevertheless follow the same paradigm as those that end in *u*. Not all nouns that end in *u* fall into the *u*-declension; some are 3rd-declension nouns such as *giefu*.

unvoiced

Consonants in which the vocal cords do not vibrate are considered voiced: "t," "p," and "f" are all unvoiced.

velar g

A "g" sound pronounced with the tongue touching the velum, or soft palate is called velar g. The "g" in "good" is a velar g.

verb

A verb is an action word. "Ruled," "wears," "carries," "to wander" and "fought" are all verbs. The verb is the action being done. In the sentence "Alfred ate the cakes," "ate" is the verb.

voiced

Consonants in which the vocal cords vibrate are considered voiced. "D," "b" and "v" are all voiced. "Ð" and "þ" may be voiced or unvoiced; compare *mūþ* and *mūÐas*.

vowel length

The duration of the pronunciation of a vowel is called vowel length. Vowels can be long or short. A macron can be used to represent a long vowel, a mini-apostrophe a short vowel.

weak adjective

Adjectives that are supported by a demonstrative (rather than standing on their own, as does a strong adjective) are considered weak adjectives.

weak noun

Nouns that end in a vowel and follow the weak nouns paradigm for declensions are considered weak nouns.

weak verb

Verbs which add an ending to a verb stem (without the vowel in the stem changing) to indicate person, number, tense, and mood are considered weak verbs.

Glossary of Old English Words

This version of the glossary is simply a compilation of all the words we have introduced in this grammar. The words have not yet been lemmatized, so they are given in the form in which they were first introduced in a practice sentence or translation exercise.

Verbs are alphabetized under their root form with any *ge* prefix given in parentheses.

> **Legend:**
>
> **adj** = adjective
> **adv** = adverb
> **conj** = conjunction
> **n** = noun
> **prn** = pronoun
> **prep** = preposition
> **v** = verb

A

ā	**adv**	always	
abbudyss	**n**	abbess	(strong, feminine)
ac	**conj**	but	
Ælfrede	**n**	Alfred	(proper noun, dative)
ǣnig	**adj**	any	
ǣr	**adv**	previously	
ætgædere	**adv**	together	
āfȳrhte	**adj**	frightened	(past participle)
āgan	**v**	to possess	(preterite-present)
ahebban	**v**	to lift, raise, exalt	(strong, Class VI)

an	**adj**	one	
and	**conj**	and	
Andree	**n**	Andrew	(masculine; Latin)
andswere	**n**	answer	(direct object; feminine accusative singular)
apostoles	**n**	apostol	(masculine, genitive)
ārǣrde	**v**	erected	(past 3rd person singular of *ārǣran*)
ardlice	**adv**	quickly	
āre	**n**	honor	(strong, neuter; dative)
āstāh	**v**	ascended	(past 1st and 3rd person singular of *āstīgan*)
āþas	**n**	oaths	(strong, masculine; accusative)

B

be	**prep**	by, on, along	
beæftan	**adv**	after	
becumað	**v**	happen, befall	(present 3rd person plural of *becuman*)
becuman	**v**	to come, arrive	(strong, Class V)
befrīnað	**v**	ask	(imperative plural of *befrīnan*)
behindan	**prep**	behind	
beorhtnys	**n**	brightness	(strong, feminine)
berȳpð	**v**	plunders	(present 3rd person singular of *berȳpan*)
(ge)bēte	**v**	repented	(past 1st and 3rd singular of *(ge)bētan*)
betȳndon	**v**	imprisoned	(past 3rd person plural of *betȳnan*)

(ge)biddan	**v**	pray to, ask	(strong, Class V)
bisceop	**n**	bishop	(nominative)
bītan	**v**	to bite	(strong, Class I)
blōdgyte	**n**	bloodshed	(strong, masculine)
blōstma	**n**	flower	(weak, masculine)
bōc	**n**	book	(radical consonant; nominative plural *bēc*)
bodade	**v**	proclaimed	(weak, 1st conjugation)
bodian	**v**	to proclaim	(weak, 2nd conjugation)
brādost	**adj**	broadest	
brōðor	**n**	brother	(radical conosonant declension; masculine)
bryne	**n**	fire, burning	(strong, masculine)
bryttigean	**v**	to share	(weak, 2nd conjugation)
būde	**v**	dwelled	(irregular verb; infinitive *būan*)
burhware	**n**	citizenry	(accusative of *burhwaru*)
būtū	**n**		both
bȳne	**adj**	cultivated	
byrne	**n**	byrnie, coat of mail	(weak, feminine)
byrnsweord	**n**	flaming sword	(strong, neuter)

C

carcerne	**n**	prison, jail	(strong, neuter)
ceastre	**n**	city, walled town	(strong, feminine; accusative)
Cerdice	**n**	Cerdic	(dative; proper name)
cilde	**n**	child	(minor; neuter)

cirdan	**v**	to turn	(weak, 1st conjugation; infinitive *cierran*)
cirice	**n**	church	(weak, feminine)
cirman	**v**	to cry out, shout	(weak, 1st conjugation)
clyppan	**v**	to embrace, love	(weak, 1st conjugation)
cohhetan	**v**	to bluster, shout	(weak, 1st conjugation)
cōmon	**v**	came	(past plural of *cuman*)
cuman	**v**	to come	(strong, Class V)
cunnan	v	to know	(preterite-present)
cwæþ	**v**	said	(past 3rd person singular of (*ge*)*cweþan*)
cymeþ	**v**	comes	(present 3rd person singular of *cuman*)
cyng	**n**	king	(strong, masculine; nominative)
cyning	**n**	king	(strong, masculine; nominative)
cyricean	**n**	church	(feminine, genitive)
cȳðað	**v**	make known	(present 3rd person plural of *cȳÐan*)

D

dæg	**n**	day	(strong, masculine; plural *dagas*)
dēman	**v**	to judge	(weak, 1st conjugation)
dēmen	**v**	would judge	(present subjunctive plural; weak, 1st conjugation)
dohte	**v**	availed	(past tense 3rd person singular of *dugan*)
dōn	**v**	to do	(irregular)
draca	**n**	dragon	(weak, masculine)

dugan **v**   to achieve,   (preterite-present)
avail

durran **v**   to dare   (preterite-present)

duru   **n**   door   (strong, feminine; accusative)

dȳre   **adj** dear,
precious

E

ēa   **n**   **river**   (strong, feminine)

ēac   **conj** also

ēage   **n**   eye   (weak, neuter)

eal   **adj** all

ealdor   **n**   lord, prince   (strong, masculine)

ealle   **adv** completely

ēaran   **n**   ears   (plural of *eare*; accusative;
weak neuter)

eard   **n**   land   (strong, masculine)

eardiaþ   **v**   dwell   (weak, 2nd conjugation)

earfoðnes **n**   hardship   (strong, feminine)

earn   **n**   eagle   (strong, masculine)

Ēastengle **n**   East Anglians   (proper name; masculine)

ēasteweard **adv** in the east

ēastrice   **n**   east kingdom   (strong, neuter)

elde   **v**   hesitated   (weak, 1st conjugation;
infinitive *ieldan*)

ēce   **adj** eternal,
everlasting

efston   **v**   hastened   (weak, 1st conjugation;
infinitive *efestan*)

eft	**adv**	afterwards	
ēow	**prn**	you, y'all, to/for you	(2nd person; plural, accusative or dative)
ēower	**prn**	your, y'all's	(2nd person; plural, genitive)
ēowic	**prn**	you, y'all	(2nd person; plural, accusative)

F

fæder	**n**	father	
(ge)faran	**v**	to travel, go	(strong, Class VI)
faraþ	**v**	go	(imperative plural of *faran*)
fela	**adj**	many	
fēoll	**v**	fell	(past 1st and 3rd person singular of *(ge)feallan*; strong Class VII)
feor	**adv**	far	
Finnas	**n**	Saami, Finns	(proper noun)
Finnum	**n**	Saami, Finns	(dative of *Finnas*)
flēon	**v**	to fly	(strong, Class II)
(ge)flīeman	**v**	put to flight	(weak, 1st conjugation)
fōð	**v**	catch, capture	(present plural of *fōn*; Class VII)
forþ	**adv**	forth	
for ðōn	**conj**	because	
for ðæm	**conj**	because	
fordrīfan	**v**	to drive away	(strong, Class I)
forgyldan	**v**	to pay for	(strong, Class III)

227

forwearð	**v**	perished	(past tense 3rd person singular of *forweorðan*)
fōt	**n**	foot	(radical consonant declension; masculine)
fyrst	**adj**	first	

G

gafol	**n**	profit, taxes	(strong, neuter)
gān	**v**	to go	(irregular)
gār	**n**	spear	(strong, masculine)
gē	**prn**	you	(2nd person; nominative plural)
gēare	**n**	year	(strong, masculine; dative)
gebytlu	**n**	building	(strong, neuter; nominative plural)
gedreccednes	**adj**	tribulation	(strong, feminine)
georne	**adv**	eagerly	
guma	**n**	man, hero	(weak, masculine)
gūðsearo	**n**	war-gear	(strong, neuter)
geaf	**v**	gave	(past 1st and 3rd singular of *giefan*)
geat	**n**	gate	(strong, neuter; accusative plural of *gatu*)
gelȳfdre	**adj**	advanced	(genitive, feminine)
gemǣne	**adj**	common to	
giefan	**v**	to give	(strong, Class V)
gif	**conj**	if	
git	**prn**	you two	(dual)
gōd	**adj**	good	

Godes	**n**	God	(strong, masculine; genitive)
gōdum	**n**	with goods	(strong, neuter; dative plural)
grǣdelīce	**adv**	greedily	
gram	**adj**	angry	
gristbitian	**v**	to gnash the teeth	(weak, 2nd conjugation)
gryþ	**n**	quarter, truce	(accusative case)
gyfe	**n**	gift	(strong, feminine; nominative *giefu*)
gȳmð	**v**	cares for	(present 3rd person singular of *gīeman*)

H

habban	**v**	to have	(weak, 3rd conjugation)
hæbbe	**v**	have	(present 3rd subjunctive of *habban*)
hæfde	**v**	had	(past tense 3rd person singular of *habban*)
hæfdon	**v**	had	(weak, 3rd conjugation)
hæfst	**v**	have	(weak, 3rd conjugation)
hǣte	**n**	heat	(strong, feminine; nominative)
hālgan	**adj**	holy	
hasupād	**adj**	grey-coated	
hē	**prn**	he	(3rd person; singular, masculine, nominative)
Heahmund	**n**	Heahmund	(proper name; nominative)
(ge)healdan	**v**	to hold, preserve	(strong, Class VII)
hēan	**adj**	poor	

hearpian	**v**	to harp	(infinitive; weak, 2nd conjugation)
hēo	**prn**	she, they	(3rd person; nominative or accusative)
heofonas	**n**	the heavens	(plural of *heofon*; masculine, nominative or accusative)
hēom	**prn**	them	(3rd person; plural, dative)
here	**n**	war, battle	(strong, masculine)
herenesse	**n**	in praise	(dative singular)
hēt	**v**	commanded	(past tense of *hātan*)
hī	**prn**	themselves	(this is a reflexive sense, but it can be nominative)
hider	**adv**	hither	
hīe	**prn**	she, they	(3rd person; single or plural, nominative or accusative)
(ge)hīeran	**v**	to hear	(weak, 1st conjugation)
him	**prn**	it	(3rd person; singular, masculine or neuter, dative)
hine	**prn**	him	(3rd person; singular, masculine, accusative)
hīo	**prn**	she	(3rd person; singular, feminine, nominative)
hīoldon	**v**	held	(past tense, 3rd person plural)
hira	**prn**	theirs	(3rd person; plural, all genders, genitive)
hire	**prn**	hers / to her	(3rd person; singular, feminine, genitive or dative)
his	**prn**	his, its	(masculine or neuter; genitive)
hit	**prn**	it	(3rd person; neuter; nominative or accusative)

hlūde	**adv**	loudly	
hond	**n**	hand	(*u*-declension, feminine)
hræfn	**n**	raven	(strong, masculine)
hrānas	**n**	reindeer	(accusative plural of *hrān*)
hrāw	**n**	corpse	(strong, neuter)
hringdon	**v**	rang	(past tense 3rd person plural of *hringan*)
hūs	**n**	house	(nominative)
hwā	**prn**	who	(interrogative, nominative)
hwæl	**n**	whale	(strong, masculine, nominative)
hwǣm	**prn**	whom	(interrogative, dative)
hwǣr	**adv**	where	
hwæs	**prn**	whose	(interrogative, genitive)
hwæt	**prn**	what	(interrogative, neuter, nominative or accusative)
hwalas	**n**	whales	(strong, masculine, plural accusative)
hwām	**prn**	whom	(interrogative, dative)
hwelc	**adj**	of what sort	
hwī, hwȳ	**adv**	why	
hwī	**prn**	who	(interrogative, instrumental, masculine or neuter)
hwon	**prn**	who	(interrogative, instrumental, masculine or neuter)
hwone	**prn**	whom	(interrogative, masculine, accusative)
(ge)hȳranne	**v**	hearing	(inflected infinitive of *(ge)hīeran*)
gehȳraþ	**v**	heard	(present 3rd person plural of *gehīeran*)

231

(ge)hȳre   **v**   hear   (plural imperative of *(ge)hīeran*)

hyrnednebb **adj** horn-beaked

I

ic   **prn**   I   (all genders)

ieldran **n**   ancestors   (strong, feminine; nominative plural)

Īfling **n**   the River Ifling   (proper name; nominative)

īglond **n**   island   (strong, neuter)

ilca   **adj**   same

in   **prep** in   (+ accusative "into", or + locative dative "in")

inc   **prn**   you two   (dual; accusative or dative)

incer **prn**   of you two   (dual; genitive)

incit **prn**   you two   (dual; accusative)

īse   **n**   ice   (strong, neuter, dative)

K

kyng   **n**   king   (strong, masculine, nominative)

L

lǣrde   **v**   taught   (weak, 1st conjugation)

(ge)lǣrdestan **adj** most learned

lǣssa   **adj** smaller

land, lond **n**   land, country   (strong, neuter)

lande **n**   land, country   (dative)

lange **adv** long, for long

lār   **n**   teaching, doctrine   (strong, feminine, nominative)

lāðgenīðla	**n**	foe, enemy	(weak, masculine)
lēoht	**n**	light	(strong, neuter)
lēasunga	**n**	false witness	(strong, feminine)
lēoht	**adj**	light, not heavy	
lētan	**v**	left	(past tense 3rd person plural of *lǣtan*)
libban, lifian	**v**	to live	(weak, 3rd conjugation)
līc	**n**	body	(strong, neuter)
licgan	**v**	to lie	(strong, Class V)
lofodon	**v**	loved	(past tense plural; from *lufian*)
longe	**adj**	long	
lufian	**v**	love, praise	(weak, 2nd conjugation)
lȳtle	**adj**	little, small	

M

mǣden	**n**	maiden, girl	(strong, neuter)
mǣgas	**n**	kinsmen	(nominative plural of *mǣg*; strong, masculine)
magan	**v**	to be able to	(preterite-present)
mann, monn	**n**	man	(minor, masculine)
mannum	**n**	men	(dative plural of *man(n)*)
Marīa	**n**	Mary	(weak, feminine)
mē	**prn**	me	(dative or instrumental)
meahte	**v**	was able	(past tense 3rd person singular of *magan*)
mec	**prn**	me	(accusative)
medu	**n**	mead (a drink)	(*u*-declension, masculine)

men	**n**	men	(dative or instrumental)
mere	**n**	lake, body of water	(strong, masculine, dative)
(ge)mētað	**v**	find	(present tense plural of [ge]mētan; weak 1st conjugation)
micclum	**adv**	greatly	
micle	**adj**	large	
micle	**adv**	much	
mid	**prep**	with	(+ dative case)
mīn	**prn**	mine	(genitive)
mōdor	**n**	mother	(*r*-declension, feminine)
mōna	**n**	moon	(weak, masculine)
mōnað	**n**	months	(strong, masculine, plural)
monn	**n**	man	(radical consonant declension; masculine)
monna	**n**	men	(genitive plural of *man[n]*)
mōrfæsten	**n**	fastness in the moors, swamp	
morgen	**n**	morning	(masculine)
mōrum	**n**	moors	(strong, masculine, dative plural)
mōtan	**v**	to be allowed to	(preterite-present)
munan	**v**	to remember	(preterite-present)
mycel	**adj**	large, great	
mynster	**n**	monastery	(strong, neuter)
mynstermen	**n**	monks	(nominative plural of *mynster man[n]*)

N

næfre	**adv**	never	
ne...ne	**conj**	neither...nor	
ne	**adv**	not	
nēaweste	**n**	vicinity, neighborhood	(strong, feminine, dative)
nēdþearf	**n**	need	(strong, feminine)
nele	**v**	does not wish	(negative of *willan*)
(ge)nīwad	**v**	renewed	(past participle of *genīwian*)
Norþhymbre	**n**	Northumbrians	(proper name; nominative plural)
norþweard	**adv**	northward	
nū	**adv**	now	
nugan	**v**	to suffice	(preterite-present)

O

of	**prep**	from	
ofer	**prep**	over	
ofslægen	**adj**	slain	(past participle acting as an adjective)
ofslēan	**v**	to slay	
Olāfe	**n**	to / for Olaf	(proper name; dative)
on	**prep**	onto, into	(+ accusative; implies movement)
on	**prep**	on, in	(+ dative; implies location)
ond	**conj**	and	
onfēng	**v**	took, received	(past 3rd person singluar of *onfōn*)

ongan	**v**	began	(past 3rd person singular of *onginnen*)
onginnan	**v**	to begin	(strong, Class III)
onwōc	**v**	awoke	(past 3rd person singular of *onwacan*; strong, Class VI)
onscuna	**v**	avoid	(weak, 2nd conjugation; imperative singular of *onscunian*)
Oswold	**n**	Oswold	(proper name; nominative)
ōðre	**adj**	other	
oþ	**prep**	until	

P

Paulīnus	**n**	Paulinus	(proper noun; Latin)

R

recce	**v**	am interested in	(weak, 1st conjugation; infinitive *reccan*)
reliquium	**n**	relic	(Latin)
rīce	**adj**	rich	
rōd	**n**	cross, rood	(nominative)
Rōm	**n**	Rome	(proper name)
ryhtfæderencyn	**n**	direct paternal ancestry	(nominative)

S

sǣmann	**n**	seaman, seafarer	(minor, masculine)
salowigpad	**adj**	dark-feathered	
Scæ	**n**	Saint	(abbreviation; Latin)

Sancta	**n**	Saint	(Latin adjective "holy" used as a noun)
scip	**n**	ship	(strong, neuter)
sceaþa	**n**	enemy, criminal	(weak, masculine)
sculan	**v**	must, to be obligated	(preterite-present)
Scyppendes	**n**	of the Creator	(genitive singular)
sē	**dem prn**	the	(masculine, singular, nominative)
(ge)seald	**v**	gave	(past participle of *[ge]sellan*)
searo	**n**	war-gear	(strong, neuter)
secg(e)an	**v**	to say	(weak, 3rd conjugation)
seledrēamas	**n**	hall-joys	(nominative plural of *seledream*)
(ge)seoh	**v**	see	(imperative sg of *gesēon*)
(ge)seted	**v**	set, place, put	(past 3rd singular of *gesettan*; weak 1st conjugation)
sige	**n**	victory	(strong, masculine)
siglan	**v**	to sail	(weak, 1st conjugation)
singan	**v**	to sing	(strong, Class III)
(ge)sittan	**v**	to settle, remain	(strong, Class V)
siþþan	**adv**	afterwards	
slǣpð	**v**	sleeps	(present 1st and 3rd singular of *slǣpan*; strong Class VII)
snel	**adj**	quick	
(ge)somnian	**v**	to assemble	(weak, 2nd conjugation)

sōna	**adv**	soon, immediately	
spēdig	**adj**	prosperous	
springan	**v**	to spring	(strong, Class III)
staþe	**n**	shore, bank	(strong, neuter, dative)
stān	**n**	stone	(strong masculine)
standeþ	**v**	stands	(present 3rd person singular of *standan*; strong, Class VI)
stōd	**v**	stood	(past 3rd person singular of *standan*)
stōdon	**v**	stood	(past tense 3rd person plural of *standan*)
stōw	**n**	place	(strong, feminine)
styredon	**v**	stirred, moved	(past tense 3rd person plural of *styrian*; weak 1st conjugation)
sum	**adj**	one	
sumor	**n**	summer	(minor, masculine)
sunne	**n**	sun	(weak, feminine)
sunu	**n**	son	(*u*-declension; masculine)
sūðrima	**n**	south-coast	(weak, masculine)
swā	**adv**	so, as	
swā swā	**adv**	just as	
sweart	**adj**	gloomy, dark, black	
swefn	**n**	dream	(strong, neuter)
swēg	**n**	sound, music	(strong, masculine)
sweostor	**n**	sister	(*r*-declension; feminine)
swift	**adj**	swift	

swȳðe	**adv**	very	
syle	**v**	give	(weak, 1st conjugation; imperative singular)
sylf	**n**	self	

T

tacan	**v**	to take	(strong, Class VI)
tēolung	**n**	tillage	(strong, feminine)
(ge)tēon	**v**	to draw, drag	(strong, Class II)
tīde	**n**	time	(strong, feminine, accusative)
til	**adj**	good	
tō	**prep**	for, to, at	(+ dative)
tōð	**n**	tooth	(radical consonant declension, masculine)
tōniman	**v**	to open	(strong, Class IV)
trēow	**n**	pledg	(strong, feminine)
Trūso	**n**	Truso	(name of a city; nominative)
tungol	**n**	star	(strong, neuter)
twelf	**n**	twelve	(number)

Þ

þā	**adv**	then	(*þā þā*, 'then when')
þā	**dem prn**	that, the	(feminine, singular, accusative)
ðǣr	**adv**	there	
ðæt	**conj**	so that	
þafode	**v**	agreed	(past 3rd person singular of *þafian*)

þe	**prn**	which	(relative particle)
þē	**prn**	you	(2nd person; accusative or dative)
þec	**prn**	you	(2nd person; accusative)
þegenas	**n**	thanes	(strong, masculine, plural)
(ge)ðencan	**v**	to think	(weak, 1st conjugation)
þider	**adv**	thither	
þīn	**prn**	your	
ðissere	**prn**	this	(genitive, feminine, singular)
ðonne	**conj**	than	
þonne	**adv**	then	
þū	**prn**	you	(2nd person; nominative)
Đurfan	**v**	to need	(preterite-present)
ðurh-slēan	**v**	to smite through	(strong, Class VI)
ðus	**adv**	thus	

U

uncer	**prn**	of us two	(dual; genitive)
uncit	**prn**	us two	(dual; accusative)
unearge	**adj**	brave	
unfriþe	**n**	un-peace, hostility	(strong, masculine)
unīeþelice	**adv**	with difficulty	
unnan	**v**	to grant	(preterite-present)
unscyldig	**adj**	un-guilty, innocent	
untrum	**adj**	unwell	
unwrītere	**n**	bad scribe	(neuter, nominative)

ūp	**adv**	up	
ūre	**prn**	of us, our	(1st person plural; genitive)
ūrne	**poss adj**	our	(accusative singular of *ūre*)
ūs	**prn**	us	(1st person; accusative)
ūs	**prn**	us	(1st person; dative or instrumental)
ūser	**prn**	of us, our	(1st person; genitive)
ūsic	**prn**	us	(1st person; accusative)
ūt	**adv**	out	

W

wagode	**v**	waved, shook	(past tense 3rd person singular of *wagian*; weak, 2nd conjugation)
wanspēdig	**adj**	poor, destitute	
wē	**prn**	we	(1st person; nominative)
weald	**n**	forest	(strong, masculine)
wearð	**v**	became	(past singular 1st and 3rd person of *weorðan*)
wel	**adv**	well	
Wendelsǣ	**n**	Mediterranean Sea	(feminine)
wendon	**v**	went	(weak, 1st conjugation; infinitive *wendan*)
(ge)weorc	**n**	defensive work, fort	(strong, neuter)
weorðan	**v**	to become, happen	(strong, Class III)
weoruldhāde	**n**	secular life	(dative)

werod	**n**	troop, company	(strong, neuter)
Westsǣ	**n**	West Sea	(proper name)
wið	**prep**	against	(+ dative; sometimes + accusative)
wilde	**adj**	wild	
willan	**v**	to wish	(irregular)
wīsdōm	**n**	wisdom	(strong, masculine)
wit	**prn**	we two	(dual; nominative)
witan	**v**	to know	(preterite-present)
wlance	**adj**	proud	
wōp	**n**	weeping	(strong, masculine)
word	**n**	word	(strong, neuter; nominative plural *word*)
(ge)worden	**v**	become	(past participle of *[ge]weorÐan*)
(ge)worht	**v**	wrought, made	(past participle of *[ge]wyrcan*)
world, woruld	**n**	world	(strong, feminine; often *weoruld*)
wracu	**n**	suffering, pain	(strong, feminine)
wrǣcca	**n**	exile	(weak, masculine, nominative)
wrōht	**n**	strife	(strong, masculine)
wudu	**n**	wood, forest	(*u*-declension, masculine)
wurþmynte	**n**	reverence, honor	(strong, feminine, dative)
wurdon	**v**	became	(past plural of *weorðan*)
wyrm	**n**	worm, dragon	(strong, masculine)

Y

yfel	**n**	evil, harm	(neuter, accusative)
ylce, ilce	**adj**	same	
ylde, ieldo	**n**	old age	(feminine, genitive)
ymb	**prep**	about, around, approximately	

BLANK PARADIGMS

First Person Personal Pronouns Paradigm

Case	Singular	Dual	Plural
Nominative			
Genitive			
Accusative			
Dative / Instrumental			

Second Person Personal Pronouns Paradigm

Case	Singular	Dual	Plural
Nominative			
Genitive			
Accusative			
Dative / Instrumental			

Third Person Personal Pronouns Paradigm

Case	Masculine	Neuter	Feminine	All Genders Plural
Nominative				
Genitive				
Accusative				
Dative/ Instrumental				

Interrogative Pronouns Paradigm

Case	Masculine	Neuter
Nominative		
Genitive		
Accusative		
Dative		
Instrumental		

Irregular Verbs

Indicative Mood

	Present	Present	Past
1st Person Singular (I)			
2nd Person Singular (you)			
3rd Person Singular (he, she, it)			
Plurals (all three persons)			

Subjunctive Mood

	Present	Present	Past
Singulars (all three persons)			
Plurals (all three persons			

Imperative Mood

	Present Only
Second Person Singular (you)	
Second Person Plural (y'all)	

Demonstrative Pronouns Paradigms

Singular Demonstrative Pronouns: The, That

Case	Masculine	Neuter	Feminine
Nominative			
Genitive			
Accusative			
Dative			
Instrumental			

Plural Demonstrative Pronouns: The, Those

Case	All Three Genders
Nominative	
Genitive	
Accusative	
Dative and Instrumental	

Singular Demonstrative Pronouns: This

Case	Masculine	Neuter	Feminine
Nominative			
Genitive			
Accusative			
Dative			
Instrumental			

Plural Demonstrative Pronouns: These

Case	Masculine	Neuter	Feminine
Nominative			
Genitive			
Accusative			
Dative			
Instrumental			

Strong Declension Adjectives Paradigms

Singular Strong Declension Adjectives Paradigm

Case	Masculine	Neuter	Feminine
Nominative			
Genitive			
Accusative			
Dative			
Instrumental			

Plural Strong Declension Adjectives Paradigm

Case	Masculine	Neuter	Feminine
Nominative			
Genitive			
Accusative			
Dative			
Instrumental			

Weak Declension Adjectives Paradigms

Singular Weak Declension Adjectives Paradigm

Case	Masculine	Neuter	Feminine
Nominative			
Genitive			
Accusative			
Dative			
Instrumental			

Plural Weak Declension Adjectives Paradigm

Case	All Three Genders
Nominative	
Genitive	
Accusative	
Dative and Instrumental	

Strong First Declension (Masculine) Nouns Paradigm

Case	Singular	Plural
Nominative		
Genitive		
Accusative		
Dative and Instrumental		

Strong Second Declension (Neuter) Nouns Paradigm

Case	Singular	Plural
Nominative		
Genitive		
Accusative		
Dative and Instrumental		

Strong Third Declension (Feminine) Nouns Paradigm

Case	Singular	Plural
Nominative		
Genitive		
Accusative		
Dative and Instrumental		

u- declension Nouns Paradigm

Case	Singular	Plural
Nominative		
Genitive		
Accusative		
Dative and Instrumental		

r- declension Nouns Paradigm

Case	Singular	Plural
Nominative		
Genitive		
Accusative		
Dative and Instrumental		

Radical Consonant Declension Nouns Paradigm

Case	Singular	Plural
Nominative		
Genitive		
Accusative		
Dative and Instrumental		

Weak Verbs: Paradigms

First Conjugation Weak Verbs, Indicative Mood:

Present Tense

Singular	
1st Person (I)	
2nd Person (you)	
3rd Person (he, she, it)	
Plural	
1st, 2nd and 3rd Persons	

Past Tense

Singular	
1st Person (I)	
2nd Person (you)	
3rd Person (he, she, it)	
Plural	
1st, 2nd and 3rd Persons	

First Conjugation Weak Verbs, Subjunctive Mood:

Present Tense

Singular	
1st, 2nd and 3rd Persons	
Plural	
1st, 2nd and 3rd Persons	

Past Tense

Singular	
1st, 2nd and 3rd Persons	
Plural	
1st, 2nd and 3rd Persons	

First Conjugation Weak Verbs, Imperative Mood:

Singular	
2nd Person	
Plural	
2nd Person	

inflected infinitive: to (stem+)

present participle: stem+

past participle: stem+

Second Conjugation Weak Verbs, Indicative Mood:

Present Tense

Singular	
1st Person (I)	
2nd Person (you)	
3rd Person (he, she, it)	
Plural	
1st, 2nd and 3rd Persons	

Past Tense

Singular	
1st Person (I)	
2nd Person (you)	
3rd Person (he, she, it)	
Plural	
1st, 2nd and 3rd Persons	

Second Conjugation Weak Verbs, Subjunctive Mood:

Present Tense

Singular	
1st, 2nd and 3rd Persons	
Plural	
1st, 2nd and 3rd Persons	

Past Tense

Singular	
1st, 2nd and 3rd Persons	
Plural	
1st, 2nd and 3rd Persons	

Second Conjugation Weak Verbs, Imperative Mood:

Singular	
2nd Person	
Plural	
2nd Person	

inflected infinitive: stem + (a few words use "anne")

present participle: stem + (a few words use "ende")

past participle: stem + (a few words use "d")

Weak 3rd Conjugation Verbs Paradigms

Weak 3rd Conjugation Verbs: Indicative Mood

Present Tense

Singular	to have	to live	to say
1st Person			
2nd Person			
3rd Person			
Plural			
1st, 2nd and 3rd Persons			

Past Tense

Singular	to have	to live	to say
1st Person			
2nd Person			
3rd Person			
Plural			
1st, 2nd and 3rd Persons			

Weak 3rd Conjugation Verbs: Subjunctive Mood

Present Tense

Singular	to have	to live	to say
1st, 2nd and 3rd Persons			
Plural			
1st, 2nd and 3rd Persons			

Past Tense

Singular	to have	to live	to say
1st, 2nd and 3rd Persons			
Plural			
1st, 2nd and 3rd Persons			

Weak 3rd Conjugation Verbs: Imperative Mood

Singular	to have	to live	to say
2nd Person			
Plural			
2nd Person			

Strong Verb Classes and Principle Parts

Class	Infinitive	3rd Person Singular Past	All Plurals Past	Past Participle
I				
II				
III				
IV				
V				
VI				
VII				

Present Tense

	Ending	Class I	Class III
Singular			
1st Person			
2nd Person			
3rd Person			
Plural			
1st, 2nd, and 3rd Persons			

Past Tense

	Ending	Class I	Class III
Singular			
1st Person			
2nd Person			
3rd Person			
Plural			
1st, 2nd, and 3rd Persons			

Subjunctive Mood

Present Tense

	Ending	Class I	Class III
Singular			
1st, 2nd and 3rd Persons			
Plural			
1st, 2nd and 3rd Persons			

Past Tense

	Ending	Class I	Class III
Singular			
1st, 2nd and 3rd Persons			
Plural			
1st, 2nd and 3rd Persons			

Imperative Mood

	Ending	Class I	Class III
Singular			
2nd Person			
Plural			
2nd Person			

inflected infinitive: to bitanne

present participle: to bitede

past participle: biten

Preterite-Present Verbs Paradigms

Present Tense

Singular	
1st Person	
2nd Person	
3rd Person	
Plural	
1st, 2nd and 3rd Persons	

Past Tense

Singular	
1st, 2nd and 3rd Persons	
Plural	
1st, 2nd and 3rd Persons	

END NOTES

1: "Rogationtide" is a church festival in which the fields and animals are blessed. It can occur any time from late May to late July, depending upon the date of Easter.

ABOUT THE AUTHOR

Michael D.C. Drout is Professor of English and Director of the Center for the Study of the Medieval at Wheaton College, Norton, Massachusetts, where he teaches Old and Middle English, Science Fiction and the works of J.R.R. Tolkien.

Printed in Great Britain
by Amazon